Physical Sciences

Physical Sciences

Curriculum Resources and Activities for School Librarians and Teachers

Amy Bain

Janet Richer

Janet Weckman

2001
Teacher Ideas Press
A Division of
Libraries Unlimited, Inc.
Englewood, Colorado

TEACHER IDEAS PRESS
A Division of
Libraries Unlimited, Inc.
P.O. Box 6633
Englewood, CO 80155-6633
1-800-237-6124
www.lu.com/tip

ISBN 1-56308-680-8

Contents

Section 1—Energy and Machines

Section 2—Matter

Section 3—Space

Introduction

The recent explosion of children's literature has drastically changed the way many educators now teach. Teachers are electing to leave many of the "basal textbooks" behind and incorporate children's literature into the classroom. Teachers are finding that these books, bursting with photographs and colorful illustrations, capture readers' interest and keep the students involved with the topic longer than traditional textbooks. The books on the market offer something for everyone, matching interests and reading abilities of the students to various books. By using children's books, students can go beyond the basic concepts a textbook presents and dive into the topic.

In addition to nonfiction, many creative fiction books are available that are artistically illustrated and cleverly written. Teachers have discovered that these books are fun to read and, often, they can be tied into a science or social studies topic. Students may find that, while studying insects, they're also reading fiction stories such as "The Very Hungry Caterpillar," who undergoes metamorphosis, or "Two Bad Ants," who are *supposed* to be collecting food for the queen and the colony. The subjects of reading and science begin to overlap, giving students more time to do both. Tie in writing activities, art projects, and hands-on activities involving insects, and the concept of "unit studies" comes alive. A unit study incorporates skills and information from several subjects and connects them in a meaningful, stimulating way.

Physical Sciences: Curriculum Resources and Activities for School Librarians and Teachers was created to provide educators with the resources they need to prepare interesting and informative science unit studies quickly and easily. Each chapter provides resources for creating a thematic unit on one specific topic. Using *Curriculum Resources* to plan a unit, teachers can easily pick and choose books and activities to match students' interests and academic abilities. Teaching multilevel classes will no longer be intimidating, and planning time will be dramatically decreased. Teachers who make use of all of the units included in *Curriculum Resources* will cover all the material contained in a standard textbook series, and much more.

Included in this book are the resources needed to prepare stimulating science units for grades K–8. Each topic includes:

1. Key Concepts (Objectives)

    A teacher must have specific goals in mind to plan appropriate activities and lessons. Each major part of *Curriculum Resources* contains a "Key Concepts" section that outlines learning objectives by age level. These "Key Concepts" were derived from studying scope and sequence statements for several school districts, examining textbooks and other printed material, and reviewing standardized tests.

    Through the use of these "Key Concepts," the teacher maintains the flexibility of determining what will be taught and how in-depth the lessons will be. These concepts serve as a guide for lesson planning.

2. Comprehensive Teaching Resources

    Books in the "Comprehensive Teaching Resources" section are in-depth resources that cover more than one unit topic. One of these books can serve as a reference guide for your unit and be used to investigate information related to the topic but not specifically covered in that topic.

3. Teaching Resources (Nonfiction Children's Literature)

In the individual subject chapters, books summarized in this subsection are written for children using text they can understand and incorporate illustrations that capture children's interest. These books can be used in place of textbooks to teach the science topic in a more stimulating manner.

Each book is designated "P" for Primary (K–2), "I" for Intermediate (3–5), or "U" for Upper (6–8) grades. These designations indicate what age level each book's text is geared toward. Each teacher can then decide how best to use a specific book in overall lesson planning. Not all books will be needed to teach the basic concepts of a topic, but the variety of books listed will give teachers the opportunity to choose books that complement their own teaching style.

4. Reading Selections (Fiction Children's Literature)

Each subject chapter includes summaries of a variety of fiction books. These books build on the science topic through engaging stories and enjoyable illustrations. Select a variety of fiction books at various reading levels for independent reading and for shared reading times as well. Not only will these fiction books reinforce reading skills, they can also be used to reinforce the science goals and the vocabulary associated with them.

5. Science Activities

A key segment of any unit study is hands-on experimenting by the student. It is important to supplement teaching resources with projects and experiments from the "Science Activities" subsection of each subject chapter. Ideas are presented for projects that actively involve the students and expand on the science topic. Choose activities that employ a variety of skills—such as research, prediction, and comparison—and incorporate other subjects such as mathematics and English.

Rather than providing page after page of worksheets, enrichment and enhancing activities challenge students to think more creatively and in-depth about the topic. The large variety of activities offered allows the teacher to choose those that most closely match the interests and needs of the students.

Most of the activities listed require the use of everyday household items. This keeps preparation time simple and costs low. Also, activities can be easily modified to different ability levels. Incorporating a few of these activities into the teaching of a subject will increase the interest level of the student and make the lesson more fun for teacher and student alike.

6. Creative Writing and Art Activities

Immediately following the science activities are subsections that expand the science topic into other subject areas. Activities are provided in the areas of reading, writing, and art. Some activities correspond to a fiction book listed in the "Reading Selections" subsection of the chapter and relate the activity to the story. Other activities stand alone and can be assigned with no prior reading required. Again, these activities can be easily modified to various ability levels and encourage creative expression and reasoning skills.

7. Additional Resources

The "Additional Resources" section at the end of each major part lists experiment books, addresses of agencies and related organizations, names of magazines, and websites that will provide teachers with more information on the unit topic. The experiment books are available from the library and provide ideas for additional experiments. With all of these resources at their fingertips, teachers should never run out of ideas!

Curriculum Resources places a variety of resources at your fingertips to plan lessons for an entire unit. If you are a person who likes to be very structured, you can write an outline for each unit, with daily lessons. If you are a flexible, go-with-the-flow type of person, you can simply pick and choose from the resources and activities as your day develops. With the variety of books and activities included, you can quickly select an activity that will engage your class for 5 minutes or 45 minutes, based on your needs.

Using *Curriculum Resources*, the process of selecting activities and resources and planning your unit can be accomplished in less than an hour. The result can be three weeks or more of lessons. After planning several units, this process will become second nature and take even less time. With unit studies, lesson planning becomes easier and teaching becomes more fun. Watch the enthusiasm for science in your classroom grow, and revive the joy of learning.

Experiments and the Scientific Method

An important part of science education is teaching children how to think "scientifically" and develop problem-solving skills. This can be done effectively through hands-on demonstrations, activities, and experiments. The "Experiment Books" subsection in the "Additional Resources" section in each major part lists books that are filled with experiments relating to the topic. In addition to these books, some books (noted with a "+") in the "Teaching Resources" subsection in each chapter also contain experiments.

Science education would be incomplete without studying different methods researchers use to make discoveries and develop new theories. Students should learn how to apply the scientific method by doing experiments themselves. Understanding this process will strengthen problem-solving skills.

Scientific research can involve a variety of techniques. Some of the methods scientists use are:

1. *Observing nature*: Learning about the life cycle of a butterfly or how average temperatures determine when crops should be planted are examples of how observing nature provides information that can be used in other areas of study.

2. *Classifying data*: By comparing and contrasting characteristics of different objects or animals, relationships can be determined.

3. *Using logic*: When a specific principle is demonstrated repeatedly, it may logically become a scientific principle of law. For example, objects with less density than water will float. Obviously, not every object in existence was tested before this principle was formed.

4. *Conducting experiments*: This is the major process for developing and proving theories.

5. *Forming a hypothesis*: Scientists may try to explain information received by creating a theory. For example, astronomers found that Uranus was not always in the position they calculated it should be. They then hypothesized the existence of another planet, and later discovered Neptune.

6. *Expressing findings mathematically*: Scientists often explain observations through the use of mathematics. For example, scientists may observe a gravitational relationship between two planets and derive a mathematical equation expressing that relationship. This equation can then be used to predict the gravitational relationship between other planets.

7. *Pure accident*: There is always the unique case of "stumbling onto a discovery." The discovery of penicillin is an excellent example.

When performing a science experiment or project, students should strive to follow a logical, scientific method. An example of the scientific method follows.

1. *Identify the problem*: What does the student want to find out or expect to learn?

2. *Develop a hypothesis*: What does the student predict will happen?

3. *Describe the procedure and materials*: What steps will be taken to try to solve the problem? What materials will be used?

4. *Record observations/data*: What happened? What results were obtained? When appropriate, data should be recorded in graph form to make it easier to determine patterns and relationships.

5. *Generate conclusions*: What can be learned from the observations made? What conclusions can be made from the data collected?

By following this scientific method, students should learn problem-solving skills and be able to identify a problem and determine possible methods to solve it. The more frequently the students perform experiments, the more familiar they will become with the scientific method. For this reason, educators should strive to include as many hands-on activities as possible in their lesson plans.

Problem-solving skills can be used in many activities included in the subject chapters. Strengthening life-long skills such as problem solving will benefit any student.

ENERGY AND MACHINES

- Key Concepts
- Comprehensive Teaching Resources
- Chapter 1: Magnets and Electricity
- Chapter 2: Light, Heat, and Energy
- Chapter 3: Sound and Communications
- Chapter 4: Machines
- Additional Resources

Key Concepts

■ Primary Concepts

Students will be able to:

1. Identify objects that are magnetic and ones that are nonmagnetic (Chapter 1).

2. Find the strongest part of a magnet within its magnetic field (Chapter 1).

3. Locate the poles of different kinds of magnets and demonstrate how like poles repel and unlike poles attract (Chapter 1).

4. Recognize materials that magnets can attract through (Chapter 1).

5. Describe how to magnetize an object (Chapter 1).

6. Discuss various uses of magnets (Chapter 1).

7. Understand that heat and light are forms of energy (Chapter 2).

8. Cite examples of sources of light and heat besides the sun (Chapter 2).

9. Classify various objects as sources of light, heat, or both (Chapter 2).

10. Recognize that fuels, friction, and the sun are three sources of heat energy (Chapter 2).

11. Understand that heat can move from one object to another (Chapter 2).

12. Demonstrate how a thermometer can measure how hot or cold an object is (Chapter 2).

13. List ways we use heat and light energy (Chapter 2).

14. Understand that things cannot be seen without a light source (Chapter 2).

15. Understand that objects that do not give off light must reflect light to be seen (Chapter 2).

16. Recognize that light-colored objects reflect light better than dark objects (Chapter 2).

17. Recognize that dark colors absorb light (Chapter 2).

18. List materials that are transparent, translucent, or opaque (Chapter 2).

19. Identify sounds in order from softest to loudest (Chapter 3).

20. Recognize that machines can aid people in moving things and help them do work (Chapter 4).

21. Identify attributes of and differentiate among a pulley, lever, inclined plane, and wheel (Chapter 4).

■ Intermediate Concepts

Students will be able to:

1. Discuss how electricity is produced (through movement of electrons) (Chapter 1).

2. Cite the two kinds of electricity and differentiate between them (static, current) (Chapter 1).

3. Decide which materials are conductors and which are nonconductors of electricity (Chapter 1).

4. Create open and closed circuits (Chapter 1).

5. Identify the four parts of an electric circuit (Chapter 1).

6. Cite parallel and series circuits (Chapter 1).

7. Show how a magnet can be used to create an electric current (Chapter 1).

8. Explain the lines of force that surround a magnet (Chapter 1).

9. Explain how electricity and magnetism are related (can be produced by a chemical reaction within a wet or a dry cell) (Chapter 1).

10. Show that electrical energy can be changed into other forms of energy such as heat and light (Chapter 1).

11. Define the kilowatt-hour as the unit for measuring how much electrical power is used (Chapter 1).

12. Understand that electricity is a useful form of energy, but can be dangerous if handled improperly (Chapter 1).

13. Define and cite examples of energy (Chapter 2).

14. Identify common forms of energy (Chapter 2).

15. Cite examples of various ways that energy can change from one form to another (Chapter 2).

16. Cite examples of kinetic and potential energy (Chapter 2).

17. Define the word *temperature* (Chapter 2).

     Identify the units of measure for temperature (Celsius and Fahrenheit).

     Read each type of thermometer.

18. Explain how heat energy is transferred through solid matter (conduction), and through liquids and gases (convection) (Chapter 2).

19. Explain the words *sound* and *vibrate* (Chapter 3).

20. Explain how sound is produced and conducted (Chapter 3).

21. Compare and predict how sound moves through different states of matter (solids, liquids, gases) (Chapter 3).

22. Explain how sound is reflected off various surfaces (Chapter 3).

23. Predict that the speed of a vibration affects the pitch of a sound (Chapter 3).

24. Understand that the magnitude of a sound is in direct proportion to its energy (Chapter 3).

25. Explain how sound travels (Chapter 3).

26. Describe how sound waves create vibrations of the eardrum and cause us to hear (Chapter 3).

27. Understand that an echo is created by reflected sound (Chapter 3).

28. Understand that some materials absorb sound (Chapter 3).

29. Explain how various animals use sound for finding food and for direction (dolphins, bats, etc.) (Chapter 3).

30. Understand what causes noise pollution (Chapter 3).

31. Explain the terms *machine, simple machine,* and *compound machine* (Chapter 4).

32. Explain and demonstrate Newton's three laws of motion (Chapter 4).

33. Discuss the law of conservation of matter/energy, citing specific examples that illustrate the law (Chapter 4).

34. Calculate the rate of motion (Chapter 4).

35. Calculate power as the rate of doing work (Chapter 4).

36. Differentiate between centrifugal and centripetal force (Chapter 4).

37. Define *energy, work,* and *power* (Chapter 4).

38. Show how a lever, an inclined plane, and a pulley work (Chapter 4).

    Give examples and explain as simple machines.

    Explain how they use energy.

39. Recognize a wheel and axle as a simple machine (Chapter 4).

40. Contrast and compare simple and compound machines. Give examples of compound machines (Chapter 4).

41. Design a simple machine (Chapter 4).

■ Upper Concepts

Students will be able to:

1. Contrast the two types of electrical charges (Chapter 1).

2. List the properties of static electricity (Chapter 1).

3. Define the properties of magnets (Chapter 1).

4. Investigate and explain the effects of one magnet on another (Chapter 1).

5. Understand magnetic fields (Chapter 1).

6. Create a simple electromagnet (Chapter 1).

7. Explain the electromagnetic spectrum (Chapter 1).

8. Understand that coal, oil, and natural gas are fossil fuels that are important sources of energy (Chapter 2).

9. Discuss problems with using fossil fuels (Chapter 2).

10. Cite examples of energy alternatives to fossil fuels (solar, water, geothermal, wind, bioconversion, nuclear) (Chapter 2).

11. Differentiate between renewable and nonrenewable resources and cite examples of each (Chapter 2).

12. Explain the two ways in which energy is released from the nuclei of atoms (Chapter 2).

13. Understand that radiant energy travels in waves (Chapter 2).

14. Explain energy conservation (Chapter 2).

15. Discuss the interchange between potential and kinetic energy (Chapter 2).

16. Compare and contrast reflection, refraction, and diffraction of waves (Chapter 2).

17. Describe how light travels and how it is transmitted through different materials (Chapter 2).

18. Explain light intensity (Chapter 2).

19. Define the speed of light and its relationship to a light year (Chapter 2).

20. Differentiate between and demonstrate reflection and refraction of light (Chapter 2).

21. Sequence colors in order within the visible spectrum (Chapter 2).

22. Cite the primary and complementary colors (Chapter 2).

23. Demonstrate the angle of reflection and of incidence (Chapter 2).

24. Create a wave model of light to demonstrate diffraction (Chapter 2).

25. Demonstrate polarized light (Chapter 2).

26. Understand that light travels in straight lines (Chapter 2).

27. Demonstrate that light can be transmitted, reflected, or absorbed when it strikes matter (Chapter 2).

28. Compare the differences among transparent, translucent, and opaque objects (Chapter 2).

29. Compare and contrast how various mirrors affect the reflection of light (convex, concave, regular) (Chapter 2).

30. Compare and contrast how different lenses affect the refraction of light (convex, concave) (Chapter 2).

31. Describe the relationship between an object's color and the light that it reflects (Chapter 2).

32. Define *pitch, sound,* and *frequency* (Chapter 3).

33. Explain amplitude and relate it to the decibel scale (Chapter 3).

34. Explain acoustics and its importance to everyday life (Chapter 3).

35. Compare the speed of sound at various temperatures (Chapter 3).

36. Describe the Doppler effect (Chapter 3).

37. Describe a wave and identify its features (Chapters 2, 3).

38. Calculate wave speeds (speed = force x wavelength) (Chapters 2, 3).

39. Demonstrate characteristics and properties of transverse, longitudinal, and standing waves (Chapters 2, 3).

40. Explain the usefulness of levers, pulleys, inclined planes, wedges, screws, and wheels and axles. Cite examples of each (Chapter 4).

41. Compute the mechanical advantages of simple machines (Chapter 4).

42. Cite examples of compound machines (Chapter 4).

43. Recite the formula for work (work = force x distance) (Chapter 4).

44. Contrast the scientific definition of *work* and common usage (Chapter 4).

45. Demonstrate an understanding of Newton's laws of motion (Chapter 4).

46. Calculate the amount of work done in a given example (Chapter 4).

47. Define *work, power, energy,* and *force* (Chapter 4).

48. Define and demonstrate centripetal and centrifugal forces (Chapter 4).

49. Understand the different forms of energy and how one form can be converted into another (Chapter 4).

Comprehensive Teaching Resources

The following table lists books that cover a wide range of topics about energy and machines. One of these books could serve as your main teaching guide while studying this unit. Each book is listed with a short summary, and the chapters in this book that it applies to are noted. The books are listed by degree of difficulty, easiest to most difficult.

BOOK AND SUMMARY	AUTHOR	CHAPTERS			
		1	2	3	4
The Macmillan Book of How Things Work (Macmillan, 1987) Explains how electricity and many simple machines are used to make everyday items work.	Michael Folsom and Marcia Folsom	X	X	X	X
National Geographic Society: How Things Work (National Geographic Society, 1983) Uses familiar objects such as pianos, hot air balloons, calculators, and bicycles to introduce the field of physics.	National Geographic Society	X	X	X	X
Everyday Things and How Things Work (Random House, 1991) An illustrated guide that shows how hundreds of machines and processes affect our everyday lives.	Steve Parker	X	X	X	X
Warwick Illustrated Encyclopedia: Science (Warwick, 1989) Looks at the world of science, from electricity to sound.	Brenda Walpole	X	X	X	
The Way Things Work (Houghton Mifflin, 1988) Explains movement, power, light and sound waves, electricity and automation, and the invention of machines.	David Macaulay	X	X	X	X
How Things Work (Time-Life Books, 1996) Text and drawings explain the workings of certain everyday items.	Iam Graham	X	X	X	X

Each chapter in this section lists reference books that focus on the specific area of energy and machines being addressed. These books can be used to complement and expand upon the basic information provided in the comprehensive resource books listed in the previous table.

The reference books in each chapter have been classified by age level to help you select those that best fit the needs and interests of your student(s).

Chapter 1
Magnets and Electricity

■ Teaching Resources

Books containing experiment(s) relating to the subject matter are marked with a plus sign (+) before and after the title.

P   +*Batteries, Bulbs, and Wires,*+ by David Glover (Kingfisher, 1995)
Uses activities and projects to show how electricity and magnets work at home and globally.

P   +*Switch on, Switch Off,*+ by Melvin Berger (Harper Trophy, 1990)
Explains how electricity is produced and transmitted, how to create electricity, the use of generators to provide cities with electricity, and the use of electricity in the home.

P   *What Magnets Can Do,* by Allan Fowler (Children's Press, 1995)
An introduction of very basic ideas about magnets and compasses.

I   +*Electricity and Magnetism,*+ by Terry Jennings (Raintree Steck-Vaughn, 1996)
Introduces the concepts of magnetism, magnets, batteries, compasses, and electricity.

I   +*Exploring Magnets,*+ by Ed Catherall (Steck-Vaughn, 1990)
Discusses magnets and how they work. Also describes the properties of magnets.

I   +*Exploring Electricity,*+ by Ed Catherall (Steck-Vaughn, 1990)
An introduction to the basic principles of electricity.

I   *Playing with Magnets,* by Gary Gibson (Copper Beech Books, 1995)
A "playful" introduction to magnets.

I   +*Science Workshop: Electricity,*+ by Pam Robson (Gloucester Press, 1993)
Explores the properties of simple circuits and inventive ways of putting them to work to make light and power.

I   *The Way It Works: Electricity,* by Neil Ardley (Macmillan, 1992)
Discusses the different elements of electricity and how we use it.

I   +*What Makes a Magnet?,*+ by Franklyn Branley (HarperCollins, 1996)
Describes how magnets work. Includes instructions for making a magnet and a compass.

I/U *Electricity,* by Tony Hooper (Raintree Steck-Vaughn, 1994)
Details major breakthroughs in the science of electricity, from magnetism to superconductivity.

I/U *Electricity—Eyewitness Science,* by Steve Parker (DK Publishing, 1992)
Discusses properties of electricity and describes how it is made and used.

I/U *The History of Electricity,* by Robert Snedden (Thomas Learning, 1995)
A look at the history of how electricity was discovered and harnessed.

U   +*Electricity and Magnetism,*+ by Robert Gardner (Twenty-First Century Books, 1994)
Describes the properties of magnets and electricity and how they are joined to power our world.

U   +*Magnet Science,*+ by Glen Vecchione (Sterling, 1995)
Relates the discovery of magnetism, discusses the principles behind it, and suggests experiments that explain how it works.

■ Reading Selections

Books marked with an asterisk (*) before and after the title are related to activities in the activity sections of this chapter.

Ben and Me, an Astonishing Life of Benjamin Franklin by His Good Mouse, Amos, by Robert Lawson (Little, Brown, 1988)
> In this book, Amos, a close friend of Benjamin Franklin, reveals how *he* was actually responsible for Franklin's inventions, discoveries, and successes. (Chapter Book)

The Electric Elephant, by Carolyn Graham (Oxford University Press, 1982)
> A book featuring various anecdotes, riddles, and jokes.

How Thunder and Lightning Came to Be: A Choctaw Legend, by Beatrice Orcutt Harrell (Dial Books for Young Readers, 1995)
> Two very large and silly birds accidentally create thunder and lightning.

The Legend of Lightning Larry, by Aaron Shepard (Charles Scribner's Sons, 1993)
> Lightning Larry changes the town into a friendly place when he shoots bolts of lightning instead of bullets.

Lightning Inside You and Other Native American Riddles, by John Bierhorst (William Morrow, 1987)
> A collection of Indian riddles.

Marta's Magnets, by Wendy Pfeffer (Silver Press, 1995)
> Although her sister calls them junk, Marta's magnet collection proves to be very helpful.

The Master Key, by L. Frank Baum (Books of Wonder, 1997)
> A young boy accidentally summons the Demon of Electricity, who gives him special electrical gifts. (Chapter Book)

Peppe the Lamplighter, by Elisa Bartone (Lothrop, Lee & Shepard, 1993)
> In a time before electricity, a poor boy, responsible for lighting the lamps, dislikes his job until one special night.

Storm in the Night, by Mary Stolz (Harper & Row, 1988)
> While sitting through a fearsome thunderstorm that has put the lights out, Thomas hears a story from Grandfather's boyhood.

The Story of Lightning and Thunder, by Ashley Bryan (Maxwell Macmillan, 1993)
   Ma Sheep Thunder and her son Ram are forced to leave their home on Earth because of Ram's mischievous deeds.

The following books are out of print, but may be available from the local library.

Bright Lights to See By, by Miriam Anne Bourne (Coward, McCann & Geohegan, 1975)
   Rival hotel owners argue about the value of electric lights.

Harry's Stormy Night, by Una Leavy (M. K. McElderry Books, 1995)
   When a big storm knocks out their electricity, Harry's family sings and tells stories by candlelight.

Michael in the Dark, by Alison Coles (EDC Publishing, 1985)
   Michael is afraid of the dark and only feels safe when the light is left on until his mother takes things in hand.

The Washout, by Carol Carrick (Houghton Mifflin, 1978)
   Christopher rows around the lake to get help when a storm knocks out all of the electricity and the telephone.

When the Lights Went Out, by Cris Baisch (G. P. Putnam's Sons, 1987)
   Sisters attempt to amuse themselves when the electricity goes out.

■ Science Activities

Static Electricity

Give the students the following instructions for creating static electricity:
- Rub a comb on a piece of wool material, then hold it close to someone's head who has *short* hair. (The hair will be attracted to the comb.)
- Rub a balloon several times on the carpet or through your hair. Now hold the balloon close to the wall. (The balloon will stick to it.)
- Take a piece of thread (about 2 feet long) and tie one end of it around a piece of dry, unsweetened cereal. Tie the other end of the thread to an object so that the cereal can hang and swing like a pendulum. Wash a rubber or nylon comb with soapy water (to get any oil off) and dry it. Rub the comb quickly with a piece of wool cloth, then slowly bring the comb close to the suspended cereal. (The cereal will be attracted to the comb.)
- Hold a piece of newspaper up against a wall. Rub it quickly, all over, with the side of a wooden pencil. (The paper will stick to the wall. If you peel up one corner of the paper and then let it go, it will cling back to the wall.)
- Cut out the shapes of two people from some tissue paper. Hang the paper images from a drinking straw, about 2 inches apart, using thread. Tie the thread around the straw and through the heads of the two paper images. Rub another plastic straw through your hair until it is charged. Rub the paper dolls with the charged straw. What happens?
- Place two thin books on a table with a 4- or 5-inch space between them. Place torn bits of paper on the table in the space. Put a piece of window glass (handle with care!) over the two books. Rub the glass briskly with a piece of silk cloth. What do you observe happening to the paper? Repeat this activity using different kinds of cloth. Ask the students: Are the results always the same?

What is occurring to make these objects attract or repel? What causes static electricity? Can you come up with some experiments of your own that would prove the theory of static electricity?

Home Electricity

Ask students to find out whether their homes have a fuse box or a circuit breaker. Ask them to explain what the difference between the two is and what purpose these boxes serve.

Make Your Own Wire

Tell students to make their own wire to use in electrical experiments, using the following instructions:

- Tear off sheets of aluminum foil that are about 12 inches wide.
- Tear off pieces of cellophane or masking tape to equal the width of the foil. Put these pieces of tape on the *dull* side of the aluminum foil as close together as possible, without having them touch.
- Cut between the pieces of tape to make strips.
- Fold the strips in half, lengthwise, so that the dull, taped side is on the *inside*. Crease the strips by running your finger down them.
- These strips can be used in place of copper wire.

Electrical Circuit

Have students make a simple electrical circuit, as follows:

- You will need about 1 foot of copper wiring, a 1.5-volt battery, and a 1.5-volt flashlight bulb.
- Wrap one end of the copper wiring around the metal base of the light bulb. Place the other end of the wiring under the battery (standing upright).
- Touch the metal point of the light bulb to the top of the battery—the bulb will light up.

Have students use this electrical circuit to perform the "conductors and insulators" experiment that follows.

Electrical Conductors and Insulators

When students have finished making the circuits described in the previous activity, have them take a paper clip and touch one end of it to the top of the battery and the other end to the metal point on the bottom of the light bulb. Ask them: Does the bulb light? Does that make the paper clip a conductor or an insulator?

Have the class repeat the experiment using the lead tip of a pencil, the wood of a pencil, and a piece of paper and determine whether each is a conductor or an insulator of electricity.

Voltage

Use the following experiment to demonstrate what additional voltage will do to an electrical light bulb:

- Tape (use masking tape) the bare end of a plastic wire (about 8 inches long) to the positive terminal of a 1.5-volt battery. Connect the other end of the wire to one terminal of a bulb holder (socket) with a light bulb in it.

- Take another 8-inch-long wire and connect one end to the negative terminal of the same battery. Connect the other end of the wire to the other terminal of the bulb holder. You have now completed a circuit and the bulb will light.

- Add a second battery to the circuit by untaping the wire from the negative terminal of the first battery and taping it to the negative terminal of the second battery.

- Using a third wire, join the positive terminal of the second battery to the negative terminal of the first battery. Ask the students to explain what happens. Does the bulb shine more brightly, or is it dimmer? (Your bulb will shine brighter if the first battery alone was not able to bring the light to its maximum wattage. If the first battery was powerful enough to bring the bulb to its maximum wattage, the brightness of the light will remain the same, even with two batteries attached to it.)

Rheostat

Do the following activity as a class, using volunteers.

- Have one student connect one end of a 6-inch piece of copper wire to the top of a battery, then wrap the other end of the wire around the metal bottom of a flashlight bulb.

- Ask a second student to place lead from a mechanical pencil (one whole piece) on a flat surface and place the bottom of the battery on one end of the lead.

- Have a third student touch the bottom of the bulb to the lead, close to the battery. The light will burn brightly.

- Then have the first student move the bulb down the piece of lead. As the students move farther away from the battery, the bulb will burn more dimly. Explain to students that this is how a rheostat (or dimmer switch) operates.

Magnetic Field

Ask a student to sprinkle iron filings (or steel wool cut into small bits) on a clear sheet of plastic, then place a magnet on the plastic. The iron filings close to the magnet cling to it, leaving a cleared space around the magnet. This cleared space defines the magnet's "magnetic field" (the area where the force of the magnet can be felt). Have students try this exercise with magnets of different shapes and sizes. Keep a record of the results.

Divide and Conquer

Do the following demonstrations for the class:

- Cut one plastic straw, one piece of paper towel, and one piece of aluminum foil (about the same size as the paper towel) into five pieces. Roll each piece of paper towel into a tight ball. Place the pieces of straw, paper towel, foil, and five metal paper clips in a pile on a piece of window screening.

- Drag a refrigerator magnet through the pile to attract anything magnetic. Ask students to name which objects attracted. Put these objects aside.

- Rub a blown-up balloon through your hair, then hold the balloon over the pile. Ask the students what objects stuck to the balloon, and why. Put these objects in a separate pile. Repeat this process to see if you attract any other objects.

- Fill a rectangular cake pan with water. Dip the screen and the objects that remain on it into the water so that the screen touches the bottom of the pan. Pick off the floating objects and put them into a third pile.

- Lift the screen out of the water. Ask the students to identify what is left on the screen. Put these objects into a fourth pile.
- Discuss with your students how a recycling company could use this same method—only on a larger scale—to separate piles of trash for recycling.

Temporary Magnet

Direct a student volunteer to make a temporary magnet out of an ordinary nail, as follows:
- Hold a magnet in one hand and the nail in the other hand. Run the nail (always in the same direction) down the magnet. Repeat this process 50 to 100 times.
- Touch the nail to a paper clip. It will cling to the nail.
- Touch the first paper clip to a second one and see if it will also cling.

Ask the class how long the paper clips will continue to cling to the nail.

A Guessing Game

- Gather as many different objects as you can find from around your house—nail, marble, spoon, pop can, small toy, rubber band, paper clip, glass jar, pin, toothpick—and bring them in to class.
- Have students predict which objects will cling to a magnet and which won't. Write down their predictions.
- Test the theories and record the results next to the guesses.

A Magnet's Strength

- Collect several magnets of different shapes and sizes and a pile of tacks, pins, or bobby pins.
- Ask a student to move the magnet toward the pile of tacks/pins, using only one pole of each magnet, and watch them cling to it.
- Have the student pull the magnet away and record how many tacks/pins stuck to each magnet. Ask the class if there is any connection between the shape and the strength of a magnet.
- Then experiment to find out where a magnet is the strongest.
- Hang a paper clip chain from the different points of a bar magnet (the north pole, south pole, and the middle). Ask the students: Which part of the magnet is the strongest (the poles)?
- Have the students try to make a paper clip chain from one pole of the magnet to the other pole. Will it work?

Magnetic Interference

- Place a paper clip on the table.
- Hold a magnet above the paper clip. Keep lowering the magnet closer to the paper clip.
- Ask the students: Does the magnet have to touch the paper clip before it sticks to the magnet? Can magnetism travel through air?
- Replace the paper clip on the table. Put a thin sheet of paper up against the magnet and lower it toward the paper clip. Ask the students if the magnet can still attract the paper clip.
- Repeat this experiment using thin sheets of plastic, cork, glass, wood, metal, and so forth.
- Finally, drop the paper clip in a bowl of water. Lower the magnet toward the paper clip. Ask the students to describe what, if anything, happens.

Magnet Races

- Give each student a magnet and five paper clips. Tell the class to lower their magnets close enough to the first paper clip to make it move (but not close enough so that the paper clip clings to the magnet).
- Have a race to see who can move their paper clips from one end of the table to the other the fastest (put down a masking tape "finish" line so everyone will know when to stop). If someone's magnet gets so close to the paper clip that the paper clip clings to it, that person must move that paper clip back to the starting line and begin again.

Magnetic North Pole

In the United States, our compass needles point north. Ask students: Why? Is the "magnetic" north pole the same as the "actual" North Pole (as determined by latitude and longitude)? Which way would a compass needle point in Australia?

Magnetic or Not?

Ask the class to imagine that someone carrying a powerful magnet entered their bedrooms. On the board, make a list of the objects that students believe would cling to the magnet. After the list is complete, ask students to take a magnet and test the objects they thought would cling. Do they? Have them also test some of the objects that they did not think would cling. Did any of them fool the students?

Two for the Price of One

Ask students to guess what would happen if you cut a magnet in half. (It would make two magnets! Each magnet would have a north and a south pole of its own.)

Magnetize Your House

Ask students to look around their houses and yards to identify objects that contain magnets or a magnetic field, then make a list of these items. Some of the following items should be on the students' lists:

the refrigerator door (a metal strip surrounds the opening and attracts the door to hold it closed)

radios

cassette players

televisions (send out electrical signals that vibrate into a loudspeaker and are changed by magnetic fields into sounds)

any toy or machine with an electric motor (magnetism helps turn the shaft of an electric motor)

a compass

cameras

microwave ovens

remote controls

Make Your Own Lightning

Tell students to shuffle their feet across a carpet while wearing leather-soled shoes, then touch a metal doorknob. Explain to them that the spark evidenced is created in the same way that lightning is. The energy created is quickly released and is easily carried by the moisture in the air.

Insulating Wire

Ask the students: What material is used to insulate wire? Why is it imperative that wire be insulated? Tell them to make a check of their homes to make sure that all the visible wires are properly insulated and in good, working condition.

It's Beginning to Look a Lot Like Christmas

Ask students to look at their Christmas tree lights (if they are not on the tree right now, maybe they can get a strand out of storage), then plug the lights in. Ask them the following questions: What happens if you remove one of the bulbs from its socket? In some strands, if one light is removed or burns out, they all go out. In other strands, if one light burns out, the others stay on. Why is this? What is the difference between a "series circuit" and a "parallel circuit"? What are the advantages of each?

Ding-Dong, Is Anyone Home?

Ask students if they know how a doorbell works and why sound is produced when the doorbell button is pushed in. (The circuit is completed when the button is pushed and it makes the doorbell ring. When the button is not being pushed, the circuit is broken and no sound is heard.)

Grounding

Ask students if they have heard that a person is safe in a car during an electrical storm, even if lightning strikes the car. Do they know why? Explain what a Faraday Cage is.

You're Grounded!

- Cut apart a cable to show the three wires inside.
- One wire will be black, red, or blue. The second wire is white.
- The third wire, which is usually green (or bare) is the ground wire. Explain the importance of the ground wire and exactly what its purpose is. (If there is a fault in the wiring, this wire takes the current safely into the ground.)

Look, No Strings!

Demonstrate the magic of levitation with this experiment that uses two bar magnets:
- Roll a piece of stiff paper (8 by 2 inches) lengthwise into a tube a little wider than your bar magnets. Tape the roll along its edge.
- Cut a thin slot (4–5 inches long) into the side of the tube at the middle.
- Stand the tube upright and put the two magnets into the tube, making sure the two north poles are facing each other. Have students watch what happens through the slot. (The two magnets will repel each other and the top magnet will appear to float in space.)
- Ask the students what will happen if you put the magnets in the tube with the south poles together.

Hot Stuff!

Have students feel the heating effect of an electric current with this experiment:

- Tell students to connect one piece of plastic-coated wire (10 inches long) to the negative end of a 6-volt battery, then take an identical wire and connect it to the positive end of the same 6-volt battery.
- Have the students then shred off some of the plastic from the unconnected end of each piece of wire to expose the metal wires inside.
- Finally, they should squeeze these two unconnected ends together between their thumbs and forefingers. The wires will begin to feel hot between their fingers.

(Be sure to use ordinary, zinc-carbon batteries for this experiment. A high-power battery will cause the wires to become too hot, and they may burn the students' fingers.)

How Repelling!

This demonstration will be successful only when the weather is very dry (when there is very little humidity).

- Rub a strip of newspaper (12 inches long by 2 inches wide) about 20 times with a piece of wool cloth.
- Lay the newspaper across a plastic ruler and then lift up the ruler.
- The ends of the newspaper (that are hanging over the ruler) will repel each other. Ask the students if they know why. (When you rubbed the newspaper with the wool cloth, the newspaper gained electrons that gave it a negative charge.)

Compasses

A Chinese scientist named, Shen Kua, made the first magnetic compass. Have students research this invention, looking for answers to the following questions: When was the magnetic compass invented? How did Shen Kua come up with the idea? How was the idea received by his peers? Then have them draw a diagram of Kua's invention and contrast it with the modern compasses used today. Discuss the disadvantages of a magnetic compass (they don't work correctly near electrical or steel machines). Ask students if they know how the modern-day gyrocompass has solved this problem. (It does not use magnetism.)

■ Creative Writing Activities

Following are instructions to give the students for various writing activities.

- It is often said, "opposites attract" when referring to people with different personality traits who like each other. Why do you suppose someone would be attracted to an "opposite"?
- Describe someone you know and like who is your opposite. In what ways are you opposites? In what ways are you the same? Write a story about how you and your friend met and how you became friends. Have your different tastes and interests ever caused a problem between you?
- What does it mean to have a "magnetic personality"? Write a letter to a friend telling about a person you know who has such a personality. What is it about this person that makes him or her so popular?
- Write a scary story (with a happy ending) about a time when you and a brother, sister, or friend were at home by yourselves and all the power went out. What happened? How did you feel? How did the situation resolve itself? (*Storm in the Night* by Stolz)
- Write a story describing how your house would look and what your life would be like (how it would be different) if electricity had not been discovered and harnessed for residential use.

- "We got on the school bus and were starting off for school when, all of a sudden, our bus started to rise into the air. We screamed and looked out of the window. Above the bus was a large sphere that seemed to be magnetic. It was pulling us up to it. . . . " Finish this story.

- Write a story about a time when you were "shocked" by some news.

- Write an action adventure story about a hero who uses lightning as his source of strength. What good does he do? How does he use his control over lightning to defeat the villains? (*The Legend of Lightning Larry* by Shepard)

■ Art Activities

Following are instructions to give the students for various art activities.

- Make magnetic puppets. Remove the lid from a shoe box and turn it upside down. Decorate the bottom of the box to resemble a landscape or a map. Construct, out of cardboard, the silhouettes of whatever figures you wish (a man, woman, girl, boy, dog, horse, etc.). Decorate the figures and make their feet out of paper clips. Place a magnet inside the shoe box directly under the figure you wish to move. As you move the magnet, the figure will move also.

- Make your own refrigerator magnet. Draw a picture of your favorite kitchen object (fruit, vegetable, spoon, plate, pitcher, etc.) and color it. (The picture should be approximately 3 inches square and made on something sturdy, like cardboard, or on regular paper that you laminate.) When your picture is finished, glue a small, flat magnet to the back of it. Now you can use your picture as a refrigerator magnet to hold your messages or other artwork that you want to display. (You can also use bread dough or hardening clay and paint it. You could mold a heart shape and paint the name of someone special on it, for a special gift.)

- Draw a picture of the family room or living room in your house. As you draw, remove everything in the room that requires electricity to work. Replace any modern electrical items with the item that would have been used before electricity was invented. (For example, replace the lamp with a candle.) Can you replace all the items in the room? What items would you have to do without? Discuss what life would have been like without the items that we take for granted.

- Although a lightning storm can be very dangerous, it can also be very beautiful. Find some pictures that illustrate the beauty of a lightning storm. Make a collage out of these pictures to exemplify "Beautiful Danger."

- Create your own artwork by making a multicolored design on a piece of paper and then coloring heavily with black crayon over the top of the design. "Scratch off" a skyline with lightning streaks in the sky above it. You can scratch off the black crayon with a coin for a thicker look, or with the tip of a pair of scissors for a thin look. Be careful not to press too hard when scratching so that you don't tear the paper.

- Place a bar magnet in the center of a piece of paper and trace around it to mark its place. Now place a compass near the magnet. Draw a short arrow from the compass to the magnet to show the direction that the compass needle is pointing. Move the compass to a different position and repeat the previous step. Continue moving the compass and drawing arrows until you have encircled the entire magnet. (The number of arrows will depend on the size of your magnet.) The arrows on your paper should form curved lines running from the magnet's north pole to its south pole. (Notice that your lines are closer together near the poles. This is where magnetism is the strongest. The lines will be farther apart away from the poles because the magnetism is weaker there.) You can repeat this exercise several times and then color the area that denotes the magnet with a primary color. Then draw over each arrow with different colors that contain the chosen primary color.

- Benjamin Franklin is said to have "discovered" electricity when he flew a kite during a lightning storm. Design a kite of your own using your favorite colors and design.
- Make posters depicting the dangers of electricity. Label each drawing with safety rules to remember. For example: "Don't stick your fingers or foreign objects into an electrical outlet."

Chapter 2
Light, Heat, and Energy

■ Teaching Resources

Books containing experiment(s) relating to the subject matter are marked with a plus sign (+) before and after the title.

P   +*Mirror Magic*,+ by Seymour Simon (Bell Books, 1991)
Discusses how mirrors work and illustrates the scientific principles involved.

P   *Read about Fuel and Energy*, by Herta S. Breiter (Raintree, 1988)
An introduction to various types of fuels and sources of energy and how we use them.

P   *Renewable Energy,* by Jacqueline Dineen (Raintree Steck-Vaughn, 1995)
Discusses different types of renewable energy such as solar, tidal, wave, geothermal, and water.

P   *Shadows, Here, There, and Everywhere*, by Ron Goor and Nancy Goor (HarperCollins Children's Press, 1987)
Describes shadows, how they are formed, why they are of varying lengths, and how they show the shape and texture of objects.

P/I *Light! A Bright Idea,* by Siegfried Aust (Lerner, 1992)
Discusses the invention and development of lamps and other light sources.

P/I *Light and Color,* by Gary Gibson (Copper Beech Books, 1995)
A look at light and color.

P/I *Sound and Light,* by David Glover (Kingfisher, 1993)
Uses activities to introduce the properties of light and sound.

P/I *Using Light,* by Sally Morgan and Adrian Morgan (Facts on File, 1994)
Discusses the physical principles of light, its functions, and integration with modern technology.

I   +*Between Fire and Ice, the Science of Heat,*+ by Dr. David Darling (Dillon, 1992)
Discusses heat and its effect on the world around us.

I   *The Challenge of Supplying Energy,* by Gail B. Haines (Enslow, 1991)
Describes how energy works, how it is developed, and the state of our energy supplies today.

I   *Energy Today: Future Sources,* by James Strachan (Gloucester Press, 1985)
Discusses the type of energy we use today to power our cities and factories and alternative sources of power for use in the future.

I *Science Today: Radiation,* by Mark Pettigrew (Gloucester Press, 1986)
Describes what radiation is, the many different kinds of it that exist today, and how we are making use of them.

I/U +*Exploring Light,*+ by Ed Catherall (Steck-Vaughn, 1990)
Text explores the sources of light, rainbows, color and light, prisms, reflections, and other properties of light.

I/U *Letting Off Steam: The Story of Geothermal Energy,* by Linda Jacobs (Carolrhoda Books, 1989)
Examines how geothermal energy is being used as an alternative energy source in other parts of the world. Contains excellent photographs and diagrams.

U *Energy,* by Robert Snedden (Chelsea House, 1995)
Follows the discoveries made in the fields of force and energy.

U *Energy Alternatives,* by Barbara Keeler (Lucent Books, 1990)
Describes the types of fuels now being used, the necessity for conserving energy, and alternative energy sources.

U *Lasers: Humanity's Magic Light,* by Don Nardo (Lucent Books, 1990)
Explains what lasers are, how they are being used, and what effects they are having on human life.

U *Optics: Light for a New Age,* by Jeff Hecht (Charles Scribner's Sons, 1987)
Describes light and optics and explores developments such as lasers, fiber optics, and holography.

■ Reading Selections

Books marked with an asterisk (*) before and after the title are related to activities in the activity sections of this chapter.

Arthur's Eyes, by Marc Brown (Little, Brown, 1986)
His friends tease him when Arthur gets glasses, but he learns to wear them with pride.

Bear Shadow, by Frank Asch (Simon & Schuster, 1992)
Bear tries to get rid of his shadow after it gets in the way when he is trying to catch a fish.

The Biggest Shadow in the Zoo, by Jack Kent (E. P. Dutton, 1983)
Goober the elephant loses his shadow.

Black Is Brown Is Tan, by Arnold Adoff (HarperCollins Juvenile Books, 1992)
The story of members of a family who delight in all the colors that make up their very special family.

Brown Bear, Brown Bear, What Do You See?, by Bill Martin Jr. (Henry Holt, 1996)
The author shows a variety of different-colored animals, and a mother, looking at the reader.

Christmas Lights, by Ann Fearrington (Houghton Mifflin, 1996)
On Christmas night, the Merriweather family drives into town to see the lights.

The Color Box, by Dayle Ann Dodds (Little, Brown, 1992)
A monkey finds a box with spots of color inside and journeys to many bright landscapes through it. Each page has a hole showing the next color.

A Color of His Own, by Leo Lionni (Dragonfly Books, 1997)
> A small chameleon is sad because he doesn't have a color of his own.

A Dark, Dark Tale, by Ruth Brown (E. P. Dutton, 1992)
> The author talks about many dark, dark places that look sinister but are not too scary because of the use of shafts of light in the pictures.

Hot-Air Henry, by Mary Calhoun (William Morrow, 1984)
> A Siamese cat stows away on a hot-air balloon and ends up having a fur-raising adventure.

The Hot and Cold Summer, by Johanna Hurwitz (Scholastic Paperbacks, 1991)
> Two 10-year-old boys discover there is room for another friend, even if it's a girl. (The sequel is *The Hot and Cold Winter,* 1988.)

Hot Hippo, by Mwenye Hadithi (Little, Brown, 1994)
> A legend of why the hippo lives in water.

I Have a Friend, by Keiko Narahashi (Aladdin, 1998)
> A little boy tells about his shadow that is with him all day long.

Let's Paint a Rainbow, by Eric Carle (Cartwheel Books, 1998)
> Colors are introduced as painters create a rainbow cat.

A Light in the Attic, by Shel Silverstein (Harper & Row, 1981)
> A collection of humorous poems.

The Light in the Forest, by Conrad Richter (Juniper, 1995)
> The story of a young boy who is taken from his parents at the age of four by Delaware Indians, raised in the forest for 11 years, then returned to his family by a military expedition. (Chapter Book)

The Light Princess, by George MacDonald (Sunburst Books, 1992)
> The story of a princess who loses her "gravity." (Chapter Book)

Little Blue and Little Yellow, by Leo Lionni (Mulberry Books, 1995)
> A story about the many colors derived from blue and yellow.

The Little Red Hen, by Paul Galdone (Houghton Mifflin, 1985)
> The little red hen finds that she must do all the work herself to get flour to bake a cake. However, her friends are more than willing to help her eat the cake.

My Teacher Glows in the Dark, by Bruce Coville (Minstrel Books, 1991)
> A student is not sure what to do when he discovers that his new teacher glows. (Chapter Book)

One Light, One Sun, by Raffi (Crown, 1990)
> Three diverse families see the "light" and, on a warm, sunny day, realize that they are not so terribly different.

Out of the Blue: Poems about Color, by Hiawyn Oram (Hyperion Books/Children, 1993)
> A collection of poems and verses about color.

Papa Lucky's Shadow, by Niki Daly (McElderry Books, 1992)
> Papa Lucky teaches his granddaughter to dance his old routines. She learns so well, she can follow his every move.

Peppe the Lamplighter, by Elisa Bartone (Lothrop, Lee & Shepard, 1993)
> In a time before electricity, a poor boy, responsible for lighting the lamps, dislikes his job until one special night.

The Pinkish, Purplish, Bluish Egg, by Bill Peet (Houghton Mifflin, 1984)
> What hatches out of a pinkish, purplish, bluish egg? It is a griffin named Ezekiel, who must win the hearts of the woodland creatures.

A *Solitary Blue,* by Cynthia Voigt (Scholastic Books, 1993)
> The gap between Jeff and his father widens when his mother reenters his life. Only love, truth, and friendship can close it. (Chapter Book)

Ten Black Dots, by Donald Crews (Mulberry Books, 1995)
> This book uses black dots to count and to depict wheels on a bus, foxes' eyes, and so forth.

Who Said Red?, by Mary Serfozo (Aladdin, reprint ed., 1992)
> A discussion between two children, one of whom is interested only in red, while the other introduces many other colors.

The Year of Fire, by Teddy Jam and Ian Wallace (McElderry Books, 1993)
> A grandfather recollects the worst fire he can remember.

The following books are out of print, but may be available at the local library.

Blue Bug's Book of Colors, by Virginia Poulet (Childrens Press, 1981)
> Blue Bug experiments with mixing colors in an attempt to make many different colors.

My Very First Book of Colors, by Eric Carle (Thomas Y. Crowell, 1974)
> Colors are introduced in a charming and interesting way.

Mom! I Need Glasses!, by Angelika Wolff (Lion Press, 1970)
> Susan finds that an eye exam doesn't hurt, and the glasses she gets help her to see better.

Return of the Shadows, by Norma Farber (HarperCollins, 1992)
> A group of shadows rebel and find new "owners."

The Rooster's Horns, by Ed Young (Collins Publishing, 1978)
> Presents the plot of a Chinese play and directions for making a theater and shadow puppets.

Spectacles, by Ellen Raskin (Atheneum, 1968)
> Iris mistakes objects around her as peculiar things (Aunt Fanny appears to be a dragon) until she is fitted with glasses.

■ Science Activities

Light and Water

Demonstrate to the class what happens to light when it passes through water:

- Place a piece of plastic wrap over a page from the newspaper. Put a few drops of water on the plastic (or better yet, use unflavored gelatin that has been mixed with water).
- Show the students the newsprint and ask them: How do the words on the newspaper appear? What does this tell us about light passing through water?

Colored Lights

- Get three flashlights. Cover the lens of one of the flashlights with red cellophane, cover the second lens with blue cellophane, and cover the third with yellow cellophane.
- Project the red and yellow lights on a white wall or a piece of white paper taped to a wall. Overlap the circles of light. Ask the students what color it makes. Can they guess why isn't orange?
- Try other combinations and record the results. Then have the students look at different colored crayons with the three flashlights and ask them: How do they appear? What conclusions can you draw about color absorption? How does this explain that mixing red and yellow paints gives a different result than mixing red and yellow lights?
- **Upper Student Challenge:** What is the difference between color addition and color subtraction?

Waves

- Have a student tie a rope (a 100-foot length works well) to a tree or doorknob, then move the rope up and down to make waves. Ask the class: Does it take more energy to make short waves or tall waves? Have various students experiment with making one wave first, then making many waves.
- This is a demonstration of amplitude and frequency. (Amplitude = height of a wave; frequency = number of waves divided by time). To demonstrate wave speed (or velocity), practice making just one wave. Have a student time how long it takes for the wave to travel from your hand to the end of the rope. (Repeat a few times times for consistency.) The speed of the wave, or velocity, equals the distance (length of the rope) divided by time.

Colors and Heat

- Have students paint six paper cups six different colors (Make sure that black and white are two of the colors.), then paint six squares of paper in the same six colors that you used for the cups. (The paper squares should be large enough to cover the open end of the cups and be secured with a rubber band.)
- The students should then pour cold water into each cup until it is half full and take the temperature of each (they should all be the same). Have students secure the colored paper square that matches the cup over the cup opening with a rubber band. Place all of the cups in the sunlight and let them sit for three hours.
- Have students check the temperature of the water in each cup every half-hour and log the results for each cup. Ask them: Which cup of water got the warmest in the shortest amount of time? Which cup of water stayed the coolest? How could this information help you decide what clothing you might want to wear on a hot or cold day?

Rainbows

- Hold a prism in the sunlight, or near a strong, artificial light. Point out to students that a rainbow forms on the wall or floor.
- Explain to students that white light is composed of many different colors. When the light passes through the prism, the rays of light are bent in varying amounts. Ask them what other material can also bend light. (They should think of the conditions present when a rainbow appears.)

Catch a Rainbow

Do the following demonstration to show the class a rainbow:
- Pour about an inch of water into a shallow tray. Put the tray by a window. Pull the curtains so only a thin shaft of light comes into the room.
- Place a mirror in the water and rest it at an angle using some modeling clay to hold it in place. Move the tray until the sunlight shines directly on the mirror.
- Move a piece of white cardboard around between the tray and the window until a rainbow reflects onto it. You may have to adjust the mirror to get it exactly right.

It's Magic

- Have a student place a spoon in a clear glass filled with water and look at the spoon from several feet away. The spoon will appear to be broken at the surface of the water. (Older students may also observe that the portion of the spoon that is underwater looks magnified. The curvature of the glass acts as a lens and causes the appearance of enlargement.) Explain to the class that the spoon appears bent or broken because the light rays refract (or bend) in varying amounts because of the different densities of air and water.
- Ask students why it is important to remember this concept when participating in activities such as spear fishing. Can they think of other areas in which this principle would be useful?

Tint Versus Color

- Have each student choose a primary color (red, blue, or yellow) and give each student some paint of that color.
- Have them experiment by placing several drops of paint on a piece of paper and adding varying amounts of black or white paint (or both!) to the primary-colored paint.
- As the students: What different colors did you make? Were you able to make pink? Orange? How? Explain how different colors and tints are made. (One color plus some white *or* some black makes varying tints. Two or more primary colors are mixed to make different colors.)

Camouflage

- Discuss what camouflage is (protective coloration) and how different animals use it to blend in with their habitats. Ask the students why it is important for animals to be able to blend in with their environment.
- To demonstrate camouflage and color, obtain a box of colored toothpicks. Separate the toothpicks so that you have 10–15 of each color. With the class, take the toothpicks outside, toss them into the air, and let them fall into the grass. See how many of the toothpicks one student can find in one minute.
- After one minute, stop the student and examine the toothpicks that have been collected. Ask the class: Was one color easier to find than the others? Which colors were more difficult to find?

Eyeglasses

- Show various pairs of eyeglasses. Ask the students to describe whether the lenses are convex or concave and explain that if the lenses are concave, objects will appear smaller. Those glasses are correcting nearsightedness. The convex lenses correct farsightedness and magnify objects.
- Ask students what bifocals are and if they know what their purpose is.

A World without Light

- Ask students what they think living in a world with no light, or being blind, would be like. Blindfold a student and instruct him or her to perform a relatively simple, everyday task (brushing teeth, pouring a glass of water or milk, etc.).
- Have the student write a summary of what the experience was like and how he or she felt in the dark.

Conducting Heat

- Discuss whether some substances conduct heat faster than others. Then set out cups or bowls made from different materials (china, aluminum, wood, glass).
- Put boiling water in each of the containers you gathered. Have a few students feel the outside of each container immediately after you add the water and record their impressions. After five minutes, have the students feel the outside of the containers again and record any change that has taken place.
- Remove the hot water and add crushed ice to each container. Have the students feel the containers after five minutes and describe what they feel like.

More Heat Conduction

Do this experiment as a demonstration for the class. You will need several different types of wire (e.g., copper, aluminum, galvanized steel, stainless steel), a candle, paper clips, waxed paper, and a stopwatch.

- Lay an 18-inch piece of wire flat on the waxed paper. Space five paper clips 1 inch apart along the wire. Drip candle wax from the burning candle onto the wire and paper clips so that the paper clips stick to the wire. Pick up the wire (you may have to scrape the wax and paper clips off of the waxed paper) and hold the tip of the end of the wire that the paper clips are closest to in the candle flame.
- With your stopwatch, time how many seconds it takes for each paper clip to fall off the wire (when the wax melts from the heat). Set a maximum time to hold each type of wire in the flame (30–40 seconds). Repeat this process twice with each type of wire. Ask the students: Which type of wire conducts heat the best? Which one(s) does not conduct heat well?
- Make a class chart or graph of your results.

Heat Retention

Demonstrate whether water, gravel, or soil retains the most heat:

- Using three glass jars, fill one with water, one with gravel, and the third jar with soil. Insert a thermometer into each.
- Have a student record the temperature of each substance at the beginning of your experiment. Then place the jars in a pan containing 1–2 inches of water. Slowly heat the water. Ask the students which jar absorbs the heat the fastest. Have a student record the changes in temperature in each jar and the time frame during which each occurred.
- Ask the students the principle established by the results of this experiment as it relates to changes in our weather (on the coasts, or near water).
- Ask the class to explain what geothermal energy is.

Soot

As a demonstration of how soot forms, light a candle, then hold a spoon in the flame for a few seconds. When you remove the spoon from the flame, there is a black substance where the flame touched the spoon. Ask the students if they know where this black substance came from. (As the candle burns, carbon (or soot) is burned away in the flame. The black material on the spoon is carbon that was removed from the flame before it had a chance to burn.)

Solar Energy

- Have a student examine the lens of a magnifying glass and identify whether it is convex or concave. Take the class outside on a sunny day with the magnifying glass and a piece of paper. Concentrate a small beam of sunlight through the magnifying glass onto the paper. After 15–30 seconds, you will see and smell smoke. If you hold the magnifying glass in this position long enough, the paper will catch on fire.
- Ask the students what the lens is doing to change the sunlight's strength and how this relates to society's attempts to harness solar power.

More Solar Energy

- Have each student fill two paper or foam cups with cold water (using the same temperature in both cups), then cover one cup with aluminum foil and add food coloring to the other cup to make the water as black as possible. Tell the class to place both cups in the sunlight.
- After 15 or 20 minutes, have students record the temperature of each cup of water. Ask them: How do they compare? In what cases would you want to reflect the sun's rays, and in what cases would you want to absorb them? Ask students to look at a solar panel used for heating homes, if possible, then describe for the class how it is constructed.

Energy and Its Sources

Have students each make three columns on a piece of paper. In the first column, they should list all the sources of energy they can think of (e.g. coal, gas, wood, sun, water, steam, wind, atomic, nuclear, mechanical, battery, electric, chemical, geothermal). In the second column, they should list how we get each type of energy or how we harness it for use. Have them give examples in the third column of how each source of energy is used in our society today.

Coal

Have the students research coal, looking for answers to the following questions:
- How is it formed? Can people make coal? Why is it important to conserve coal and investigate alternative energy sources?
- How is coal mined? What is the biggest health problem associated with mining coal? What are some of the safety precautions miners must take? What are the ecological concerns associated with mining coal?
- Which states mine the most coal? Which countries mine the most coal? What are some coal products?

Then have students write a research paper covering any, or all, of this information.

People and Energy

Many sources of energy exist in our society, and many occupations depend on this energy. With the class, make a chart with three columns. In the first column, list various occupations. In the second column, list the energy source(s) they require for their job. In the third column, list how they use this energy. (Encourage students to think of other occupations that they would like to chart.)

Eye Talk

Explain to the students that light is reflected differently through different lenses, which is why eyeglasses are custom made for each individual person. Ask them: What is the difference between an optometrist, optician, and ophthalmologist? What duties does each perform?

Which Way Did It Go?

You can show that light travels in straight lines. This experiment works best at night, so ask students to do it at home, with someone's help. They will need a flashlight, a piece of thick black paper, a pin, and some tape. Give them the following instructions:

- Make a hole in the middle of the black paper with the pin. (The paper needs to be large enough to fit completely over the front and extend over the edges of the flashlight lens.) Tape the paper over the lens of the flashlight.
- Turn off all the lights and turn on the flashlight. The light will shine only through the pinhole. Take off the paper. The flashlight now lights up a larger area.

Explain to the students that if rays of light didn't travel in straight lines, the light coming through the pinhole would spread out and light up a larger area of the room.

Demonstrate How a Reflecting Telescope Works

- On a sunny day, leave the curtains or blinds open slightly (about 4 inches).
- Take a mirror with a curved surface (one that magnifies your image) and point the mirror toward this gap in the curtains. Keep changing the angle of the mirror until it accurately reflects onto your wall what is directly outside the window.
- Explain to the students that the mirror has just collected light rays from outside, focused them, and reflected them onto the wall, just like a reflecting telescope. This is how astronomers look at the stars.

Watch Convex Lenses Refract Light

Demonstrate refraction for the class, as follows:

- You will need a piece of cardboard (about 4 by 6 inches). Cut two thin slits (about 2 inches long, about 1/2 inch apart, and no more than 1/16th inch wide) in the cardboard.
- Fill a glass jar or bottle with water and add a few drops of milk. Set the jar about 6 inches from the edge of a table.
- Place some modeling clay on the edge of the table directly behind the jar. Stand the cardboard up in the clay so it is behind the jar.
- Turn on a flashlight and turn off the lights. Shine the flashlight through the slits in the cardboard in the direction of the bottle.
- The milky water causes the light rays from the slits to come closer together. It focuses them as a converging lens would.

- Have one student hold the flashlight and have another student stand so that his or her eye is where the two rays meet. Tell the student to look back at the flashlight, then describe his or her observations.

I See the White Light!

- Have each student trace a circle around a can or a lid on a piece of strong, white cardboard, then draw lines to divide the circle into three equal sections, going outward from the center (as in cutting a pie).
- Then have them paint one section yellow, one section red, and the third section blue; let the paint dry; then cut out the circle.
- Ask the students to use the point of a pencil to make two holes in the cardboard, one on each side of the center of the circle.
- Students should thread a string (about 24 inches long) through the holes and tie the ends together. (They will have a loop on each side of the circle.)
- Tell them to hold one loop in each hand and twist the string until it is tightly wound on both sides of the circle.
- Finally, they should pull their hands apart sharply so that the string unwinds and then winds back up again, causing the color wheel to spin around. Ask them what color they can see as the wheel spins (white), and why? (There are equal amounts of the three primary colors on the wheel. They see this combination as white light.)

■ Creative Writing Activities

Following are instructions to give the students for various writing activities.

- Write a humorous story about someone who loses his or her glasses and encounters numerous mishaps while trying to manage without them. What kinds of situations does this person get into? How does he or she make out? (*Mom! I Need Glasses!* by Wolff)
- What does it mean when someone tells you, "You are the light of my life"? Write a letter to your mother, father, sister, brother, or close friend and explain why he or she is the light of your life.
- Light has always been associated with goodness, happiness, and laughter, whereas dark is seen as sinister, evil, and foreboding. Write a short essay explaining why you think this is the case. Make two lists immediately after your essay. In one column list "light" sayings/phrases. In the other column, make a list of "dark" sayings/phrases. (*A Dark, Dark Tale* by Brown)
- "Cindy had been feeling sad all day. She had been moping around the house looking dejected. Her mother wondered what was bothering her, but Cindy told her it was nothing. Then, the doorbell rang. Cindy went to answer it. As Cindy opened the door, her face lit up. . . ." Finish the story in your own words.
- Write a "colorful" story. Pick a topic (picnicking in the park, hiking up a mountain, going to the circus) and try to use as many colors in your descriptions as possible. How many did you use? Can any of the other students think of any more? (*Blue Bug's Book of Colors* by Poulet)
- Take out a notebook or a piece of paper. When the teacher says the name of a color, you have 30 seconds (or 15 seconds, or 45 seconds depending on what the teacher tells you) to write down as many things as you can think of that are that color. You will get points either for each accepted word that you have written down or only for the words that you wrote that no one else playing the game thought of. (Incorporate math into the game by having the students keep track of their own scores and by having them compare their scores.)

- Make up a poem about your shadow in which you attempt to explain what your shadow is and what, if any, use it is to you. Be imaginative! (*Bear Shadow* by Asch; *Papa Lucky's Shadow* by Daly)

- You have just discovered coal! Write an informative pamphlet to send out to residential and commercial concerns describing the advantages and disadvantages of your discovery.

- You have been asked to participate in an experiment testing solar energy. You and several colleagues will be living for the next six months in a test city powered entirely by solar energy. Many new inventions will be tried here for the first time. Write journal entries for the first two weeks of your stay in which you describe all the wonderful inventions you have seen and your reactions to them and to the project.

- Collect as much information as you can on nuclear power and its uses. (Write to government agencies, get books from the library, and write to activist groups for and against the use of nuclear energy.) After you have completed your research, write a newspaper article detailing your views on the nuclear power issue.

- Gather information on the flight of the *Enola Gay* (the airplane that dropped the first atomic bomb on Japan). Pretend that you were assigned to the *Enola Gay* for this mission. Write a letter home to a family member telling how you felt before and after this historic mission.

- Imagine that you are living before the invention of the light bulb and before electricity was used to light and heat homes. Write a short story telling what an evening would be like spent at home with your family without any electric lights or conveniences (*Peppe the Lamplighter* by Bartone). Then imagine that you were alive during the time when Edison invented the light bulb and was trying to convince people of its worth. Write a newspaper article either championing his invention or denouncing it.

- Write a short play that could be carried out by shadow puppets. (*The Rooster's Horns* by Young)

- Write a story describing what you would do if you discovered that your teacher glowed. (*My Teacher Glows in the Dark* by Coville)

■ Art Activities

Following are instructions to give the students for various art activities.

- Make your own eye chart using pictures rather than letters. The top picture should be the largest, and each subsequent row of pictures should be a little smaller than the one above it. You can give your eye chart a theme (using similar pictures) or use any pictures that you like. (Depending on the age of your students, use the eye charts in a game in which the children must tell what letter the object depicted in each picture begins with or how the name of the picture is spelled.)

- In the Bible, Joseph is said to have a "coat of many colors." Create your own coat by drawing a picture of a coat and then coloring it with your favorite colors. You can also glue swatches of different colored and patterned material to your coat instead of coloring it.

- Design your own pair of eyeglasses. Make sure they fit your particular personality. Would your glasses be wild, funny, glamorous, or studious (*Spectacles* by Raskin)? Cut pictures out of magazines of some of your favorite personalities. Draw glasses on the ones who don't have them or decorate the glasses of personalities who already wear them. Try to make the glasses outlandish or amusing.

- Make a shadow picture by cutting out the shape of an object (e.g., a car) first from a piece of colored paper and then from a piece of black paper. On a plain, white piece of paper, design a background for the objects you have cut out (e.g., a city scene). Then paste the black object and the colored object on the background you have created. Place the black object behind the colored one and let it "peek" out 1/4 inch or so to create the illusion of a shadow.

- Using a magnifying glass, look closely at several everyday objects around you, such as a paper towel, a leaf, or your skin. Draw a picture of what the object looks like under the magnifying glass. On a separate piece of paper, draw what the object looks like to the naked eye. After making several sets of drawings, bind them in a book. Place the picture depicting the object under a magnifying glass first, then follow it with the picture of the object as it really looks. See if others can guess what the object is by looking at the magnified picture. They can then turn the page to see if they guessed correctly.

- On a piece of paper, make several black dots (any size). Create a picture that incorporates these black dots. (*Ten Black Dots* by Crews)

- Make a silhouette of yourself: Shine a bright lamp on a piece of black paper that is taped to the wall. Stand between the wall and the lamp so that your shadow appears on the paper. Have another person trace your silhouette with chalk on the black paper. Cut out the silhouette and paste it on a piece of brightly colored paper.

- Place a bright light so that it shines directly on the wall. Practice making shapes with your hands so that the resulting shadows look like different animals. Pick a favorite animal story (e.g., *The Three Little Pigs, Goldilocks and the Three Bears, The Ugly Duckling, Charlotte's Web*) and put on a "shadow" play using your hands to make the different characters.

- Look at several pieces of art by famous artists (e.g., Rembrandt, Van Gogh, Picasso, Monet). You can check out books on art from the library, look through the encyclopedia, or, better yet, visit a local art museum. How does the artist use color and light? Where are the focal points? How do dark paintings make you feel, as opposed to bright, bold paintings? How do the paintings reflect the time period and/or life of the artist (*The Color Box* by Dodds)? Try to copy a painting of one of the artists you admired most. How does your painting compare to that of the artist? Create your own unique painting that reflects your personality. What colors are predominant in your painting? In what style is your painting done?

- Draw a picture of how you think Holland looked during the time that windmills were used as the major source of power. What did the countryside look like dotted with windmills?

- People are often said to be "energetic." Draw an energetic picture in which the people, animals, and even objects seem to be actually moving.

- Find a picture in an encyclopedia or library book of the geyser Old Faithful. Using different-colored chalks and cotton balls, make your own geyser. You can make your picture on a piece of colored construction paper or make an entire scene by gluing twigs, grass, leaves, and so forth to a landscape you have drawn with colored pencils.

- Design your own animal that hatches from a wildly colored egg. (*The Pinkish, Purplish, Bluish Egg* by Peet)

- Select several colorful items from around your house, then experiment with mixing different colors of paint to see if you can make the different shades that match the colors of the selected items. You can also try to match the color(s) of a favorite flower growing in your yard. (*Let's Paint a Rainbow* by Carle)

Chapter 3
Sound and Communications

■ Teaching Resources

Books containing experiment(s) relating to the subject matter are marked with a plus sign (+) before and after the title.

P   *Hearing*, by Henry Pluckrose (Gareth Stevens, 1995)
A basic introduction to hearing, with easy-to-read text and colorful photographs.

P   *Hearing Things*, by Allan Fowler (Children's Press, 1991)
Discusses the sense of hearing and how it expands our world.

P   +*Sound Experiments*,+ by Ray Broekel (Children's Press, 1983)
Easy-to-read text discusses sound, pitch, sound waves, vibration, frequency, and length.

I   *The Ear and Hearing,* by Steve Parker (Franklin Watts, 1989)
Discusses the ear, how it receives sounds, and how it transfers these sounds to the brain.

I   +*Hearing Sounds,*+ by Gary Gibson (Copper Beech Books, 1995)
Experiments and activities that explore the concept of sound.

I   +*The Science Book of Sound,*+ by Neil Ardley (Harcourt Brace Jovanovich, 1991)
Simple experiments demonstrate basic principles of sound and music.

I   +*Sound and Music,*+ by Kay Davies (Steck-Vaughn, 1992)
Focuses on how sound is produced, transmitted, and received. Activities are included that explore sound recognition, dynamics, and pitch variation.

I   +*Sound Science,*+ by Etta Kaner (Perseus Press, 1991)
Explores sound through experiments, riddles, interesting facts, puzzles, and games.

I/U +*Exploring Sound,*+ by Ed Catherall (Steck-Vaughn, 1990)
Explores sound and how it travels, how the human ear receives it, and how it can be recorded.

■ Reading Selections

Books marked with an asterisk (*) before and after the title are related to activities in the activity sections of this chapter.

A Button in Her Ear, by Ada Litchfield (Whitman, 1987)
   A little girl humorously misunderstands what others are saying, until her hearing deficiency is detected and she gets a hearing aid.

The Country Noisy Book, by Margaret Wise Brown (HarperCollins, 1994)
> A little dog goes to the country and hears the sounds of many animals.

Do Not Disturb, by Nancy Tafuri (William Morrow, 1987)
> A wordless book about a family camping in the woods who unwittingly disturb the woodland creatures during the day. At night, the creatures have a surprise of their own.

Frog Is Frightened, by Max Velthuijs (Tambourine Books, 1995)
> Strange noises in the night frighten Frog and his animal friends.

The Hee-Haw River, by Dee Lillegard (Henry Holt, 1995)
> Annoyed when the farmer's wife complains about its murmur, the river sets in motion a confusing chain of events.

The Hungry Thing Goes to a Restaurant, by Jan Slepian (Scholastic, 1995)
> Hungry Thing eats in a restaurant and asks for many interesting things to eat while the waiter tries to figure out what he means.

I Hear a Noise, by Diane Goode (Unicorn Paperbacks, 1993)
> A little boy hears noises at his window at night and is frightened. As it turns out, he has every right to be frightened.

Joshua's Night Whispers, by Angela Johnson (Orchard, 1994)
> Joshua and his father listen to the night sounds.

The Listening Walk, by Paul Showers (HarperCollins, 1991)
> A little girl and her father take a quiet walk, identifying sounds as they go.

Lizard Music, by D. Manus Pinkwater (Bantam Books, 1996)
> After being left to take care of himself, Victor meets a community of intelligent lizards and learns of an invasion from outer space. (Chapter Book)

Morning Sounds, Evening Sounds, by Cecile Schoberle (Simon & Schuster Books for Young Readers, 1994)
> A child listens to a variety of sounds during the day, from Mom's wake-up call to a kitten's bedtime purr.

Mr. Brown Can Moo, Can You?, by Dr. Seuss (Random House, 1989)
> Presents the wonderful sounds that Mr. Brown can make and wonders if the reader is also able to make these sounds.

Music, Music for Everyone, by Vera B. Williams (William Morrow, 1988)
> Rosa earns money by playing in the Oak Street Band to help with expenses while her grandmother is sick.

My Five Senses, by Aliki (Harper Trophy, 1990)
> An easy-to-read presentation of the five senses and how we use them.

Nobody Listens to Andrew, by Elizabeth Guilfoile (D. C. Heath, 1990)
> Andrew tries to tell his family and others about the bear asleep in his bed, but nobody has time to listen.

The Noise Lullaby, by Jacqueline Ogburn (Lothrop, Lee & Shepard, 1995)
> Describes the noises a child hears at night before falling asleep.

The Noisemakers, by Judith Caseley (Greenwillow, 1992)
> Two mothers find the perfect place for two noisy, active children to play.

Noisy Nora, by Rosemary Wells (Puffin, 2000)
> A little mouse makes a lot of noise trying to be noticed by two very busy parents.

Oh What a Noisy Farm, by Harriet Ziefert (Tambourine Books, 1995)
> All the farm animals get into the act when a bull starts chasing the cow around the pasture.

The Pattaconk Brook, by James Stevenson (Greenwillow Books, 1993)
> Frog and snail follow the brook to the sea in search of all the different noises it makes.

Peeping and Sleeping, by Fran Manushkin (Clarion Books, 1994)
> Barry and his father take an evening walk, exploring the strange peeping sounds they hear.

Poems Go Clang!, by Debi Gliori (Candlewick Press, 1997)
> A collection of noisy short poems.

Polar Bear, Polar Bear, What Do You Hear?, by Bill Martin Jr. (Henry Holt, 1991)
> Children imitate the sound of many of the zoo animals for the zookeeper.

The Thing That Bothered Farmer Brown, by Teri Sloat (Orchard, 1995)
> Farmer Brown and the farm animals are ready for sleep, but a tiny, whiny sound keeps them awake.

Thump, Thump, Rat-a-Tat Tat, by Gene Baer (HarperFestival, 1996)
> A marching band grows larger and louder as it nears, and then softer and smaller as it goes away again.

Thunder Cake, by Patricia Polacco (Paper Star, 1997)
> When a storm approaches her grandmother's farm, a little girl learns not to be afraid of thunder by helping Grandmother make her famous Thunder Cake.

Too Much Noise, by Ann McGovern (Houghton Mifflin), 1967
> Peter goes to the village wise man to see what can be done about all the noise around his house.

"Uh-Oh!" Said the Crow, by Joanne Oppenheim (Bantam Books, 1993)
> On a dark, windy night, the farm animals are frightened by strange noises and think a ghost is in the barn.

A Very Noisy Girl, by Elizabeth Winthrop (Holiday House, 1991)
> Elizabeth's mother gets a break from her very noisy girl when Elizabeth pretends to be a dog.

What Noise?, by Debbie MacKinnon (Dial Books for Young Readers, 1994)
> Brief text and photographs introduce some of the sounds made by things in the world of young children.

When the Woods Hum, by Joanne Ryder (Morrow Junior Books, 1991)
> A little girl listens in awe to the sound of the cicadas, then returns 17 years later with her son to hear them again.

Whisper Goodbye, by Dorothy Nafus Morrison (Troll, 1992)
> When Katie learns that she must move from her small town in Oregon, she also must face the fact that she cannot take her pet horse to her new home. (Chapter Book)

■ Science Activities

Shoe Box Symphony

Take a shoe box without the lid and place rubber bands of different lengths and thickness around it, widthwise. Pluck the different rubber bands. Ask the students:

- How do the pitches compare? Which have a higher pitch: the shorter bands or the longer ones? The tight bands or the loose ones? The thin bands or the thick ones? Why?
- Must an object vibrate to create sound? Can a rubber band make a sound when it is not vibrating?
- Place your hand on your throat and hum. What do you feel? Must your voice box vibrate to create sound?
- (Turn the box over and pluck the rubber bands.) Why does the sound stop so quickly? (There is no room for the rubber bands to vibrate.)

Sound Absorption

- Have students knock on a table or floor with their fists, then repeat the activity, this time place something soft, such as a pillow, on the surface. Ask them how the sound changed, and why.
- Ask the students: What objects in your home absorb sound (e.g., carpet, draperies, and soft furniture)? What kinds of objects does sound bounce off of (e.g., walls, hardwood floors, and wood furniture)?

Speechless

- Try to communicate an idea without talking or writing. Write various sentences (e.g., "Let's go outside.") on individual index cards. Have the students choose a card and try to convey the idea without talking. Ask them: How difficult was it? How did it make you feel? Were you frustrated? Tell them to write a short summary of what it was like to be without sound for communicating.
- Have students wear earplugs for part of a day, then ask them: Was everyday life more difficult when you weren't able to hear as you are used to? How did it make you feel?
- Ask students to make a list of changes they would make in their surroundings and their actions if they had someone who was hearing-impaired staying with them for several days.

What Does It Sound Like?

Have students make an audiotape of different sounds around their houses and neighborhood, then play the tape for other family members or classmates and see if they can guess what the sounds are.

Kazoo

Students can make a kazoo by placing a square of waxed paper over the end of a cardboard tube and securing it tightly with a rubber band. They should poke a hole in the tube, then hum into the tube and feel the vibration.

Ask the students to experiment with different sounds by covering and uncovering the end of the tube with their hands and covering and uncovering the hole in the tube. They can even decorate their kazoos to personalize them.

Sign Language

Get a book from the library and teach the students a few phrases of sign language. See if they are able to communicate, through sign language, with other family members or classmates.

Good Vibrations

Show students how to "see" a vibration. Lay one end of a ruler or knitting needle on the end of a table, letting the other end hang out in mid-air. Hold the end that is resting on the table with one hand, and snap the end that is hanging out with your other hand. Try extending the ruler to varying distances (3 inches, 6 inches, 9 inches). Ask students to describe how the sound changes. Have a student feel the air directly above the ruler you just snapped; he or she should feel the air moving.

How Fast Is Sound?

Explain to the students that it has been determined that sound travels at 1,100 feet per second. Using this fact, how can they determine how far away lightning is? Tell them that the lapse between the time when we see the lightning and when we hear the thunder determines how far away a storm is. When they see the lightning, they should start counting slowly: "1, 2, 3." Each second counted before they hear the thunder represents a distance of 1,100 feet. Therefore, if they count five seconds between seeing lightning and hearing thunder, the storm is approximately one mile away.

Radio Bands

- Most radios have two bands: AM and FM. Ask the students: What do those initials stand for? How do the sound waves vary in AM and in FM? Have students research radios and how the two different frequencies came into being and how they work.
- Explain to the students that AM waves vary in amplitude and FM waves vary in frequency. If they travel in a car, one band (FM) fades out before the other (AM). One way for them to remember this is to compare sound waves with light waves. For example, ask them which they could detect better from a far distance, a light that changes its brightness or a light that changes its blinking pattern? (Similarly, changes in amplitude (AM waves) are recognized for a longer distance than changes in frequency (FM).)

Silent TV

Ask students to watch a favorite television program with the sound off, then write down what they think the story was about. They should have someone who watched the program with the sound on tell them what it really was about (or they can tape the program on a VCR). Have them compare what happened to their versions.

Sound and Solids

- Can sound travel through a solid object? Have a child place his or her ear on one end of a tabletop. Tap on the other end of the table with a pencil. Could the child hear the sound? Repeat the tapping with the child's ear off the tabletop. Ask the child: Did the tapping sound the same? Which was louder? Why do you suppose that, in Western movies, people put their ears on the railroad tracks or on the ground?
- Inflate a balloon by blowing into it and fill another balloon with water. Have students hold the balloons up to their ears and tap on the balloons. Discuss how sound waves travel through solids, liquids, and gas.

I See That Sound!

Have the students each stretch a piece of clear plastic tightly over the top of a jar and use a rubber band to hold it in place, then sprinkle a small amount of salt or sugar over the plastic, spreading it out evenly. They should then hold a metal tray or the tip of a cookie tin close to the jar and bang it somewhat loudly with a spoon. Point out how the grains "dance" over the plastic as they hit the tray, because of the sound vibrations moving through the air.

Great Inventors

Sound is transmitted in many ways today, thanks to inventors who constructed items such as the telegraph, telephone, radio, and phonograph. Have each student choose one invention that aids in communication and research the inventor, looking for answers to the following questions: When did the inventor make a first model? What gave the inventor the idea for the invention? Did the inventor profit from the idea? How was the invention accepted by society? How has the invention changed our lives over the years?

Who Said What?

- Turn on a radio and tune it in-between stations so that you can hear a station but there is a great deal of static along with it. Ask students to decipher what is being said on that station and write down a summary of what they hear.
- Students should compare their stories with those of the other students. They will probably discover that each arrived at a different idea or noticed different details.
- Tell students that it is easy to misinterpret a topic or become misinformed when we do not hear all of what is being said. This often happens with the hearing-impaired. Ask them how they felt when they couldn't understand all that was being said? Did they find themselves "filling in the gaps"?

Low and Loud

Have students get their parents' permission to do the following experiment at home: Take the front cover off the speaker for a stereo, television, or radio. Turn on some loud music and watch the "cone" (the woofer) vibrate back and forth. What type of sounds caused more vibration—the high-pitched ones or the lower-pitched ones (low)?

Tell the students that the hearing-impaired population can often hear low-pitched sounds in speech (the vowels, b, d, g, m, n,) better than high-pitched sounds (s, t, p, k).

Morse Code

Have students reproduce the Morse code on a poster and write a message to a friend in Morse code. They should see if their friends can interpret the message using the poster for reference. They can also try to make a verbal Morse code message by verbalizing the dots and dashes.

A Heliograph

A heliograph is an instrument that reflects the sun to send a code. By tilting a mirror so that it catches the sun's rays and then reflects the rays toward the person on the receiving end of the message, you can send a message using Morse code.

- Have two students stand across the street from each other. Each of the students should have a small, pocket-sized mirror. Using short flashes of light for "dots" and longer flashes for "dashes," the children can send messages to each other in Morse code.

- Students can also do this exercise at night using an Aldis lamp. (This special light has a shutter that moves up and down to block the light and create dots and dashes to send messages.) Have them make a version of the Aldis lamp by using a small piece of thick cardboard and moving it up and down in front of a flashlight to make dots and dashes.

Catch a Wave

Have students make megaphones using the following directions:

- Cut out a triangle from stiff cardboard and fold one corner across to the other. Curve it around until the two sides meet to form a cone. Tape the edges together and cut off the point to make a hole. Form another cone in the same way to create an ear trumpet. Go outside to a large open area with a friend. Stand facing each other and move a good distance apart. Yell to your friend. He or she needs to keep stepping backwards until he or she can no longer hear you shout. Mark this distance with a stone.
- Repeat the process, but this time have your friend cup both hands behind his or her ears. Can your friend go as far, or farther than, the stone marker and still hear you shout?
- Shout through your megaphone. Will your voice carry even farther?
- Have your friend use the earphone by holding it up to his or her ear. Does this make any difference?

Be a Sound Wave

To duplicate the process of sound-producing movement within our ears, do the following experiment with the class:

- Write the names of the parts of the ear on 3-by-5-inch cards. Tie a separate piece of string through the upper corners of each card to make a necklace. The cards you will need are Outer Ear, Ear Canal, Eardrum, Malleus, Incus, Stapes, Oval Window, Cochlea, and Hearing Nerve.
- Have each child wear a necklace and stand next to each other, in the order listed above, holding hands.
- A "leader" should squeeze a "message" into the first child's hand (one long squeeze, then one short squeeze, or whatever the leader chooses).
- Each child should then, in turn, transfer the message to the next person in line. (See if the correct message makes it all the way through the line of children.)

Explain to the students that this is the same process our ears go through every time we hear a sound. To help the students understand what happens in the ear of a person who is hearing-impaired, repeat the process above, but have one of the children step out of line so that the line is no longer joined. Point out that the message cannot complete the normal path because one of the parts is not working.

Make a String Telephone

Have students make string telephones. They will each need two empty plastic cups and some strong, thin string (8–12 feet). They should make a small hole in the bottom of each cup, thread one end of the string through each hole, then tie a knot on the inside end of the string to keep it in place. They should pull the string taut and speak into and listen through the cups. Tell them to make sure that the string is stretched tight as they talk. The cup acts as both the mouthpiece and earpiece. Ask them how the voice of the person on the other end gets to them at their end.

Field Trip

Check with a local audiologist to see if you can visit his or her office. Ask the audiologist to show how someone is tested for a hearing aid or even show the bones of a student's middle ear. Be sure to ask the audiologist about the "cone of light" and see if students have healthy eardrums.

High Pitch or Low Pitch?

Demonstrate pitch using the following experiments:

- Fill six test tubes (or pop bottles) with water. Each one should be filled to a different level. Set the test tubes in a rack. Tap each tube gently. Ask the students how the pitch varies. (The tube with the least amount of water has the highest pitch.)

- Blow into the tubes to make a sound. Ask the students how the pitch varies now. (The tube with the least amount of water has the lowest pitch.) Can the students explain why this is the opposite of the results you got above?

- Explain to the students that in the first experiment, the sound waves are traveling through the water, so the *lower* the water level, and the higher the pitch. In the second experiment, the sound waves are traveling through the air. The tubes with less water had *more* air to travel through, so the pitch was *lower*.

■ Creative Writing Activities

Following are instructions to give the students for various writing activities.

- You were fast asleep one Saturday morning when, all of a sudden, you heard the most peculiar noise! Where was it coming from? What was causing it? Write a diary entry for the end of that Saturday that tells "Dear Diary" what happened. (*I Hear a Noise* by Goode)

- Pretend that you work for an ear, nose, and throat doctor. The doctor has asked you to help him prepare a pamphlet to give out to his patients informing them of how they should take care of their ears. Research the proper method of caring for and protecting our ears. Design a pamphlet that will communicate this information to the doctor's patients.

- How would being deaf change your life? Research a famous deaf person (e.g., Helen Keller, Beethoven, Marlee Maitlin, William (Dummy) Joy, Laurent Clerc, Thomas Hopkins Gallaudet, Julliette Gordon Law) and write a paper about the accomplishments of that person's life. How did being deaf make this person's accomplishment harder to achieve? Was there any way in which deafness actually helped this person?

- Write a suspense story in which the detective solves a puzzling mystery through clues that involve sounds.

- Dogs can hear high-pitched sounds that cannot be heard by the human ear. Write a story in which a dog "saves the day" when it hears something that the people around it could not hear.

- You are the pilot of a helicopter that carries people back and forth to a tropical island for vacations and business. It is always very noisy in the helicopter and, therefore, nearly impossible to talk to your passengers and be heard. Design a simple, concise handout that you can give to your passengers that explains to them how you will communicate any information they will need (points of interest during the trip, emergency information in case of accident or illness, safety information).

- Imagine that you have just regained your hearing after an accident that left you deaf. What sound do you think would be the most beautiful to you? Would there be any sounds that annoy you? Write a story telling about this event in your life. Do you think this experience would change the way you live in any way?

- There are many everyday items or events that require hearing to be effective, such as an alarm clock, a fire alarm, calling out signals at a football game, or using a telephone. Research special assistive devices and services (such as message relay services) available to the hearing-impaired population. Write a letter to your congressional representative persuading him or her to contribute funds for purchasing such equipment for the hearing-impaired children in your community.

- A difficult situation for a hearing-impaired person who relies on lip reading is to be part of a conversation involving several people talking. It is hard to keep up with who is talking. Often, by the time the person figures out who is talking, he or she has missed the beginning of what was said. Write up a guide of suggestions or clues to keep in mind when a hearing-impaired person is in your group. (Suggestions: Only one person talk at a time; point to yourself when you're going to begin talking; be sure the hearing-impaired person is looking at you before you begin speaking.)

- Humans often do not think about the noise they make when in quiet places such as a park or forest and how nocturnal animals may react. Write words to the story *Do Not Disturb* by Tafuri, in which the nocturnal animals face that problem.

- You've probably heard of Seeing Eye dogs for the blind, but have you heard of hearing dogs for the hearing-impaired? These dogs are specially trained to assist an independent hearing-impaired person or couple living alone. They alert their owners to auditory cues, such as a baby crying or someone knocking at the door. Find out more about a hearing dog's training and write a news article about how these dogs serve humanity.

■ Art Activities

Following are instructions to give the students for various art activities.

- Draw a "noisy-looking" picture. Then turn the paper over and draw a "quiet" picture on the back. Which one do you like the best? (*Noisy Nora* by Wells; *The Noisemakers* by Caseley)

- Look at different types of musical instruments. Try to determine what is vibrating in each instrument to allow it to make sounds. Then look up the information about the instruments in the encyclopedia or a library book to see if you are correct. See if you can group similar instruments together into "sections" (e.g., vibrating strings, reeds, bars, surfaces, or air columns).

- Design and decorate your own telephone out of clay, cardboard, or plastic. What shape will you make your phone? What part of the phone will you talk into? Where do you put your ear?

- Get several pieces of paper and some art materials (paints, markers, and crayons). Listen closely to a piece of music the teacher will play, then draw a picture that illustrates how the music sounded to you. On the back of the picture, record the name of the piece of music that was played. Listen to a variety of pieces that vary in tempo, rhythm, and style and depict each of them. This would be a good project to bind in a book for a keepsake. You can add to the collection at any time.

- Design a musical instrument. It could be something that shakes (morocco-style), something that is plucked (harp-style), something that is banged on (drum-style), or something that is blown into to make sounds (comb with waxed paper). (This is a great activity to do to emphasize using "recyclables" that are found around the house.) Create as many different sounds as you can. Be sure to discuss what it is that is vibrating in each instrument to make its unique sound. Go wild! (*Music, Music for Everyone* by Williams)

- Find information on Alexander Graham Bell and his invention of the telephone. With the other students, put together a short play that depicts the scene in Bell's laboratory when the telephone was used for the very first time. Put on the play for other classes. (The play can be as simple or intricate as the students' age levels dictate.)

- Purchase a finger-spelled alphabet stamp set and create a greeting card or special message using the stamps. (See "Additional Resources" for availability from Evergreen.) Decorate your card and practice the message yourself using your finger-spelling skills.

- Make a "split" book of sounds. Cut three or four sheets of 8 1/2-by-11-inch paper into quarters (4 1/4 by 5 1/2 inches). On several sheets of paper draw a picture of an object or animal that makes a sound. On the other sheets write the words that depict the sound. Along the left side staple all of the pictures together, then staple the words together in the same way. Then take a full piece of 8 1/2-by-11-inch paper and fold it in half, lengthwise, to make a cover. Insert the booklet of pictures in the top half and the word booklet in the bottom half of the cover. Staple the cover so that the booklets are held in placein the cover. Flip the words or pictures and create humorous situations.

- Watch your favorite television shows with the closed captioning feature turned on. Notice the words chosen for sounds that occur in the show that aren't observable on the screen. Create captions for a video that you have at home. Write your captions on strips that fit on the bottom of your television. Turn off the sound and play your video while reading your captions. Present your "show" to someone who has not seen the video before. Did this person get a different impression of the story than you did when you heard it with the sound?

Chapter 4
Machines

■ Teaching Resources

Books containing experiment(s) relating to the subject matter are marked with a plus sign (+) before and after the title.

P   *On the Go,* by Ann Morris (Lothrop, Lee & Shepard, 1990)
Discusses how people all over the world travel from place to place by wheels, water, and so forth.

P   *Tools,* by Ann Morris (Lothrop, Lee & Shepard, 1992)
Photographs and simple text introduce tools we use to make our lives easier.

P   *Tools,* by Venice Shone (Scholastic, 1990)
Labeled pictures of all kinds of tools and related articles (with a glossary) explain the use of some tools.

P/I +*Bathtubs, Slides, Roller Coaster Rails: Simple Machines That Are Really Inclined Planes,*+ by Christopher Lampton (Millbrook Press, 1991)
Explains what inclined planes are and how they work for us, using simple text and colorful illustrations.

P/I *Machines,* by Robin Kerrod (Benchmark Books, 1996)
Examines simple machines, engines, and machines at work.

P/I *Make Way for Trucks,* by Gail Herman (Random House, 1990)
Describes different types of trucks and the jobs they do.

P/I +*Marbles, Roller Skates, Doorknobs: Simple Machines That Are Really Wheels,*+ by Christopher Lampton (Millbrook Press, 1991)
Explains how a wheel works to make work easier for us, using simple text and colorful illustrations.

P/I *Sailboats, Flagpoles, Cranes: Using Pulleys as Simple Machines,* by Christopher Lampton (Millbrook Press, 1991)
Explains what a pulley is and how pulleys work for us, using simple text and colorful illustrations.

P/I +*Seesaws, Nutcrackers, Brooms: Simple Machines That Are Really Levers,*+ by Christopher Lampton (Millbrook Press, 1991)
Explains what levers are and how they work for us, using simple text and colorful illustrations.

I/U +*Machines,*+ by Mark Lambert and Alistair Hamilton-MacLaren (Bookwright Press, 1991)
Demonstrates the principles underlying the technology of machinery through projects for building 15 different types of machines, including a water clock, screw pump, wind machine, and data sorter.

■ Reading Selections

Books marked with an asterisk (*) before and after the title are related to activities in the activity sections of this chapter.

An Auto Mechanic, by Douglas Florian (Mulberry Books, 1994)
    Simple text takes us through the daily work of an auto mechanic.

The Bear's Bicycle, by Emilie Warren McLeod (Little, Brown, 1986)
    A little boy and his favorite bear have a very exciting bicycle ride.

Bicycle Race, by Donald Crews (Greenwillow Books, 1985)
    The numbered order of a bicycle race changes as the race goes on.

The Caboose Who Got Loose, by Bill Peet (Houghton Mifflin, 1971)
    Tired of always being last in line, Katy Caboose wishes for a way to escape from the noisy freight train.

A Carpenter, by Douglas Florian (Greenwillow Books, 1991)
    Simple text takes us through the daily work of a carpenter.

Death of the Iron Horse, by Paul Goble (Aladdin, 1993)
    A group of Indians derail and rob a train in an act of defiance against the white man taking their land.

Fox on Wheels, by Edward Marshall (Puffin Books, 1993)
    Fox baby-sits for his little sister, learns to climb a tree, and wins a shopping cart race.

The Grandpa Days, by Joan W. Blos (Aladdin, 1994)
    When Phillip visits his grandpa for a week, they work on a special project together.

The Little Engine That Could, by Watty Piper (Puffin Books, 1999)
    The Little Blue Engine helps a trainload of toys and special food get over the mountain to the boys and girls waiting on the other side.

Little Toot, by Hardie Gramatky (G. P. Putnam's Sons, 1992)
    Little Toot must conquer his fear of the sea to save a big ocean liner during a storm.

Machines at Work, by Byron Barton (Thomas Y. Crowell, 1997)
    Workers at a construction site use many different machines to knock down a building and start constructing a new one.

Mike Mulligan and His Steam Shovel, by Virginia Lee Burton (Houghton Mifflin, 1978)
    An Irish steam-shovel operator refuses to desert his faithful steam shovel, Mary Anne, for a newer model.

Mr. Gumpy's Motor Car, by John Burningham (HarperCollins, 1993)
    Mr. Gumpy and his human and animal friends pile into his car to go for a ride.

The Polar Express, by Chris Van Allsburg (Houghton Mifflin, 1985)
    A little boy rides a magical train to the North Pole on Christmas Eve.

Samuel Todd's Book of Great Inventions, by E. L. Konigsburg (Atheneum, 1991)
    A little boy describes how simple inventions such as mirrors, belts, and mittens make our lives better.

School Bus, by Donald Crews (Greenwillow Books, 1984)
> Follows the progress of buses that are taking students to school and bringing them home again.

The Signmaker's Assistant, by Tedd Arnold (Dial Books for Young Readers, 1992)
> A signmaker's assistant, who has always dreamed of having his own shop, stirs up the whole town when he is left in charge by himself.

Soup on Wheels, by Robert Newton Peck (Alfred A. Knopf, 1998)
> Soup and Rob try to win the prize for best costume at their town's Spring Costume Contest. (Other "Soup" books are available.) (Chapter Book)

Truck, by Donald Crews (Greenwillow Books, 1993)
> Follows the journey of a truck as it loads and unloads.

Trucks, by Byron Barton (Thomas Y. Crowell, 1994)
> Presents many different trucks and tells what they do through easy text and illustrations.

Trucks, by Anne Rockwell (E. P. Dutton, 1992)
> The author introduces many different trucks and explains their purposes.

Wheels on the Bus, by Paul O. Zelinsky (Dutton Children's Books, 1990)
> Book version of the classic song tells of the wheels, wipers, and people getting off and on the bus.

Where's That Bus?, by Eileen Browne (Simon & Schuster, 1991)
> Mole and Rabbit are constantly distracted and keep missing the bus that will take them to lunch with squirrel.

The following books are out of print, but may be available at the local library.

Alistair's Time Machine, by Marilyn Sadler (Prentice-Hall, 1986)
> Alistair's time machine takes him on many adventures through history. Unfortunately, Alistair cannot prove this to the judges at the science fair.

Big Wheels, by Anne Rockwell (E. P. Dutton, 1986)
> Introduces many different wheels on working vehicles and shows their purposes.

Five Secrets in a Box, by Catherine Brighton (E. P. Dutton, 1987)
> Virginia, Galileo's oldest daughter, wonders about the things she finds on her father's work table, especially a soft, white feather.

Handy Hank Will Fix It, by Anne Rockwell (Henry Holt, 1988)
> As Handy Hank goes about his job of fixing things, he gets to see many other people doing their jobs also.

Mr. Murphy's Marvelous Invention, by Eileen Christelow (Clarion Books, 1983)
> Mr. Murphy makes a housekeeping machine for his wife's birthday, but the family is shocked to find out what the machine really does.

Mrs. Armitage on Wheels, by Quentin Blake (Alfred A. Knopf, 1987)
> Tells of the misadventures of Mrs. Armitage who keeps making more and more complicated changes in her bicycle.

My Very First Book of Tools, by Eric Carle (Thomas Y. Crowell, 1986)
> Pages split so readers can find the proper combination of words and pictures.

Tin Lizzie, by Peter Spier (Doubleday, 1975)
> Describes the experiences of a Model T car that has a series of owners from 1909 to the present.

Train Whistles, by Helen Roney Sattler (Lothrop, Lee & Shepard, 1985)
> Explains how train whistles are used as signals and tells what some of these signals mean.

Wheels Away, by Dayle Ann Dodds (Harper & Row, 1989)
> A runaway wheel takes a bump, noisy ride through town.

■ Science Activities

Levers

Set up a lever by placing a plank on a small cylindrical object such as a pencil. Tie a string to an object and place the object on one side of the lever. Have the students try to lift the object, first by pulling up on the string, then by pressing down on the other side of the lever. Ask them which uses more energy and which was easier (i.e., used less energy).

More Levers

- Set up a lever by placing a plank on a cylindrical object. Place an object, such as a book, on one end of the lever. Have the class count the number of blocks that you must place on the other end of the lever to balance the objects.
- Move the cylinder closer to the book and try the experiment again. Then move the cylinder farther away from the book. Ask the students how moving the cylinder changes the number of blocks required to balance the lever.

Classifying Levers

- Tell students that levers can be divided into three classes. A Class 1 lever has the fulcrum between the weight and the force (e.g., a seesaw). If the weight is between the fulcrum and the force, it is a Class 2 lever (e.g., a nutcracker). A Class 3 lever has the force between the fulcrum and the weight (e.g., tongs).
- Have each student take a piece of paper and make three columns, labeling them "Class 1," "Class 2," and "Class 3." The students should determine into which class each of the following objects falls when used in the described activity and write the activities in the appropriate columns:

    Cutting paper with a scissors (1)

    Using tweezers to remove a splinter (3)

    Opening a door (2)

    Pulling a nail out of a board using the claws of a hammer (1)

    Using a wheelbarrow to move dirt (2)

    Moving a rock with a crowbar (1)

    Eating with a fork (3)

    Using a pencil or pen to write (3)
- What other examples can students think of for each category?

Inclined Plane

- Bring in several objects from around your house (e.g., a ball, pencil, empty soda pop can, unopened can of vegetables, roll of masking tape, blocks, plastic cup). Set up an inclined plane (or ramp).
- Ask the students to predict which of the objects will go the farthest when rolled down the inclined plane. Then roll each object down the inclined plane and have students measure how far each rolls. Ask them which objects rolled the farthest and what characteristics they share.

Mechanical Versus Electrical

- Have students cut out pictures of objects that use mechanical energy (hand-operated can openers, egg beaters, food grinders, pencil sharpeners, bicycles, manual typewriters) and ones that use electrical energy (electric can openers, electric mixers, toasters, electric typewriters, blenders).
- Ask the students to name simple machines that are used for mechanical energy.
- Have them make charts and glue the pictures of the objects they found that use mechanical energy on one side and the pictures of objects that use electrical energy on the other side. Ask them if they found any machines that use both.

Pulley

Have the students do the following activity and answer the questions:
- Make a pulley by running a string through an empty spool of thread. Tie both ends of the string to fixed objects so that the spool is held in mid-air.
- Tie a heavy object onto another string.
- Lift the object up by the string and observe how heavy the object feels.
- Wind the string over the pulley and pull the string down to lift the object. Is it easier to lift the object this way?
- How can pulleys be used in everyday life?

Force/Pressure

- Drive a nail through a thin board. Set the board on a table so the pointed end of the nail sticks up. Place a balloon on the nail. Place a brick on top of another board and position both on top of the balloon. Before letting go of the board, ask the students to predict what will happen when you do. Then let go of the board. (The balloon will pop because the force of the brick and board are all applied at one point of the balloon.)

  Repeat this experiment, but have about 20 nails sticking up through the board (placed about 1/2 inch apart). Ask the students to predict what will happen this time when you let go. (The balloon won't pop because the force of the brick and board is spread over more nails. The pressure is less.)

- Have students try to slice a ripe tomato with the flat side of a knife. (The tomato will squash because the force of the knife is spread over too big an area.) With adult supervision, have them use the sharp side of the knife. (The tomato will be easy to slice because all the force is concentrated on a small area of the tomato.)

Ball Bearings

- Have the students place two unopened cans of equal size on top of one another, then try to spin the top can around.
- Then have them place several marbles between the cans and try to spin the top can again.
- Ask them why it is easier to spin the can the second time. (The marbles serve as ball bearings and reduce friction.)

■ Creative Writing Activities

Following are instructions to give the students for various writing activities.

- Write a rhythmic tune that would be fun to sing while on a seesaw.
- You have been given the chance to take the first trip in Professor Whatnot's Time Machine. What time period would you travel to? Keep a journal describing what you see and what happens to you during your journey. (*Alistair's Time Machine* by Sadler)
- Your neighbor has invented a flying car. She has told you about her invention but is keeping it secret from everyone else because she is afraid that someone will try to steal her idea. One night, as you are getting ready for bed, you look out the window and see someone lurking around outside your neighbor's garage. You rush down the stairs and sneak out the back door. Make up your own ending to this adventure.
- Invent a labor-saving device that would help you with one of the chores that you do around the house. Describe what the device looks like, how it works, and what task it is meant to do. Draw a picture of the device to go along with the description.
- In the days before the automobile was invented, people traveled using horses or went on foot. When the automobile was first seen on the streets, many people felt that they were extremely dangerous and should be banned from use. Put yourself in these people's place. Do some research about the first automobiles (how they were constructed, how fast they could go as compared to the horse, what traffic rules existed) and write an impassioned newspaper editorial condemning this new "menace" to society.
- Create an ad for the newspaper advertising a machine that you are trying to sell to the public. Remember that ads must include a lot of information in a limited amount of space. So keep it short and to the point.
- Simple machines have enabled the handicapped to become more mobile. Imagine what it would be like to spend a day in a wheelchair trying to accomplish your regular daily activities. Write a journal or diary entry for the end of such a day, describing the problems you encountered and whether you were able to overcome them.
- Many historians believe that the only way that the Egyptians could have built the pyramids and the Sphinx was to use simple machines to help move the huge blocks of stone they used. Today, the job would be much easier. Write a memo to your supervisor outlining the course of action you plan to take to complete work on the pyramids within the deadline the supervisor gave you. Include details of the equipment you will use to accomplish the task.
- Write a proposal to the principal of your school requesting new playground equipment. In your request, describe what the equipment would be like and what simple machines are incorporated in it. Be as descriptive as possible, using lots of adjectives.
- You have just invented a special gadget for a secret agent to use. What does your gadget do? What does it look like? Write a detailed description of your invention that includes its name, its purpose, its description, and instructions for its proper use. You could also include a detailed drawing of the device with each part labeled.

■ Art Activities

Following are instructions to give the students for various art activities.

- Draw a blueprint for a new machine you have invented. What would your machine be able to do? How would it look? Do you have a name for your invention? Write a short explanation of what your new machine is used for. Write an advertisement for your machine that would convince others to buy it.

- On a saucer, cookie sheet, or aluminum meat tray, place two or three paper towels (to serve as a blotter). Place several dabs of paint (as many different colors as you want), several inches apart, on the paper towel. Run the tires of a toy car or truck through the paint (one color at a time, or mix the colors) and then make a picture out of the wheel tracks on a piece of white paper. (*Fox on Wheels* by Marshall; *Trucks* by Barton)

- Draw a picture of two animals on a seesaw. Do your animals weigh the same, or are they different sizes? What has to be done to the seesaw to adjust for any weight difference? Draw other animals involved in other activities on the playground. Draw a piece of playground equipment that could be considered an inclined plane (a slide).

- Draw a picture in which you make everything out of circles and wheels. Find different wheels or circles around the house and trace around them. What kinds of things can you make out of circles (e.g., a snowman, flowers, a mouse's face, a bear's face, a turtle). (*Wheels Away* by Dodds; *Big Wheels* by Rockwell)

- Design your own flying machine. Write an explanation of how it works beneath the picture. Label all the parts of the machine.

- Make a drawing in which you combine two (or more) existing tools into one tool that accomplishes many tasks. Give your tool a name. Write a short description of your tool to use in advertising it to the public.

- Several companies today are developing electric cars. Design your own model of an electric car, name it, and write an advertising slogan for it. (*Tin Lizzie* by Spier)

■ Experiment Books

Blinkers and Buzzers, by Bernie Zubrowski (Morrow Junior Books, 1991)
> Presents experiments and projects designed to reveal aspects of electricity and magnetism.

Energy, by Larry White (Millbrook Press, 1996)
> Readers learn about the properties of energy through simple experiments.

Experimenting with Magnetism, by Alan Ward (Chelsea Juniors, 1991)
> Explores magnetism through experiments and projects.

Experiments with Electricity, by Helen J. Challand (Children's Press, 1986)
> Contains experiments related to the properties of electricity and introduces different kinds of batteries.

Experiments with Light and Mirrors, by Robert Gardner (Enslow, 1995)
> Contains experiments using mirrors and other simple materials usually associated with play.

Experiments with Magnets, by Helen J. Challand (Children's Press, 1986)
> Contains experiments that introduce magnets and magnetism and demonstrate the magnetic field and the properties, strength, and uses of magnets.

The Magnet Book, by Shar Levine and Leslie Johnstone (Sterling, 1997)
> Provides instructions for 30 simple experiments exploring magnets and electricity.

Magnets, by Janice Van Cleave (John Wiley & Sons, 1993)
> A collection of science projects and experiments using magnets.

Magnets and Electricity, by Alan Ward (Franklin Watts, 1992)
> Uses simple experiments to demonstrate the properties of magnets and electricity.

Physics for Kids: 49 Easy Experiments with Electricity and Magnetism, by Robert W. Wood (TAB Books, 1990)
> Contains 49 simple experiments pertaining to electricity and magnetism.

Physics for Kids: 49 Easy Experiments with Optics, by Robert W. Wood (TAB Books, 1990)
> Contains 49 experiments on subjects such as how the eye pupil adjusts for light, how light travels in a straight line, light diffraction, and how to build a kaleidoscope.

The Thomas Edison Book of Easy and Incredible Experiments, by James G. Cook (John Wiley & Sons, 1987)
> Simple experiments, activities, and projects on electricity and magnetism compiled by The Thomas Alva Edison Foundation.

■ Additional Reading Material

Benjamin Franklin: The New American, by Milton Meltzer (New York: Franklin Watts, 1988)

Benjamin Franklin, Scientist and Inventor, by Eve B. Feldman (New York: Franklin Watts, 1990)

Communication Satellites, by D. J. Herda (New York: Franklin Watts, 1988)

Helen and Teacher, by Joseph Lash (New York: Delacorte Press, 1980)

The Importance of Benjamin Franklin, by Gail B. Stewart (San Diego: Lucent Books, 1992)

Lewis Howard Latimer, by Glennette Tilley Turner (Englewood, N.J.: Silver Burdett, 1991)

The Man Who Dared the Lightning, by Thomas Fleming (New York: William Morrow, 1971)

Samuel Morse, by Mona Kerby (New York: Franklin Watts, 1991)

Save That Energy, by Robert Gardner (New York: Messner, 1981)

The Story of My Life, by Helen Keller (New York: New American Library, 1988)

Thomas Alva Edison, by Vincent Buranelli (Englewood, N.J.: Silver Burdett, 1989)

Thomas Alva Edison, by Christopher Lampton (New York: Franklin Watts, 1988)

Thomas Edison: The Great American Inventor, by Louise Egan (Chicago: Children's Press, 1987)

The Three Lives of Helen Keller, by Richard Harrity (New York: Doubleday, 1962)

■ Organizations

General

American Gas Association
1515 Wilson Blvd.
Arlington, VA 22209

American Petroleum Institute
Publications & Distribution Section
1220 L St., NW
Washington, D.C. 20037

Atomic Energy Clearinghouse
1325 G. St., NW
Washington, D.C. 20037

Edison Electric Institute
Educational Services
90 Park Ave.
New York, NY 10016

Exxon Company
P. O. Box 2180
Houston, TX 77001

National Coal Association
Educational Division
1130 17th St., NW
Washington, D.C. 20036

National Science Teachers Association
1742 Connecticut Ave., NW
Washington, D.C. 20009

Shell Oil Company
1433 Sablier Circle W Dr.
Indianapolis, IN 46239

Union Carbide Corporation
Public Affairs
1730 Pennsylvania, NW
Washington, D.C. 20006

U. S. Department of Energy Office of Education,
Business & Labor Affairs
613 G. St., NW
Washington, D.C. 20037

Hearing-Impaired

Evergreen
P. O. Box 20003
Alexandria, VA 22332
Finger-Spelled Alphabet Stamp set

Gallaudet College Bookstore
Gallaudet College
Washington, D.C. 20002

National Association of the Deaf
814 Thayer Ave.
Silver Spring, MD 20910

■ Web Sites

The following Web sites reference additional Web sites relating to the topic. These Web sites were created especially for children. All sites were accessed in March 2001 and were active at that time.

Airplanes and flying: http://www.yahooligans.com/science_and_oddities/Machines/airplanes_and_flying

Boats and ships: http://www.yahooligans.com/science_and_oddities/Machines/boats_and_ships

Inventions: http://www.yahooligans.com/science_and_oddities/Machines/inventions

Robots: http://www.yahooligans.com/science_and_oddities/Machines/robots

Technology: http://www.yahooligans.com/science_and_oddities/Machines/Technology

The following web sites discuss specific topics related to energy and machines:
Audio Illusions: http://www.philomel.com/

Electricity: http://www.mos.org/sln/toe/toe.html

Laser Shows: http://www.laserium.com/

Lasers and holography: http://www.enter.net/~holostudio

National Public Radio: http://www.npr.org/

Public Broadcasting Service: http://www.pbs.org.welcome.html

Solar House: http://solstice.crest.org/renewables/wlord

Sound activities: http://www.alpcom.it/hamradio

Sound Basics: http://jcbmac.chem.brown.edu/scissorsHtml/sound/charOfSound.html

SECTION 2

MATTER

- Key Concepts

- Chapter 1: Mass and Measurement

- Chapter 2: Physical and Chemical Changes

- Additional Resources

Key Concepts

■ Primary Concepts

Students will be able to:

1. Explain the term *matter* and understand that all objects take up space and have weight (Chapter 1).

2. Differentiate among solids, liquids, and gases, identifying examples of each (Chapter 1).

3. Understand that, although air is invisible, it takes up space and has weight (Chapter 1).

4. Observe that weight is not always directly related to size (Chapter 1).

5. Compare weights of various objects and predict which of two objects would be heavier (Chapter 1).

6. Understand that items that are heavier than water will sink, and items that are lighter than water will float (Chapter 1).

7. Understand that metric units (centimeters, milliliters, and meters), as well as standard American units, can be used to measure length, volume, and mass (Chapter 1).

8. Understand that some things can change from one state of matter to another (Chapter 2).

■ Intermediate Concepts

Students will be able to:

1. State the definition of *matter* (Chapters 1, 2).

2. Explain the differences among elements, compounds, and mixtures (Chapter 1).

3. Establish that all matter contains properties that can be detected by certain senses (physical properties of matter: color, odor, size, shape, hardness, density) (Chapter 1).

4. Demonstrate that different substances have differing levels of densities (Chapter 1).

5. Review metric units, showing that they can be used to measure matter (Chapter 1).

6. State the definition of mass and describe its relationship to volume (Chapter 1).

7. Understand that matter contains chemical properties that will affect its reaction to other substances (Chapter 2).

8. Explain the difference between physical and chemical changes, citing examples of each. (Physical change is a change in shape, size, or state of matter. Chemical change takes place when one or more different kinds of matter are formed.) (Chapter 2).

■ Upper Concepts

Students will be able to:

1. Differentiate between mass and weight (Mass stays constant, but the weight of an object depends on gravity.) (Chapter 1).

2. Identify and discuss the physical properties of various items (Chapter 1).

3. Explain what an element is (a substance made of only one kind of atom) (Chapter 1).

4. Explain the current scientific model of an atom (Chapter 1).

5. Understand that elements are classified in the periodic table according to common properties and be able to show how to test acids, bases, and salts (Chapter 1).

6. Differentiate between an element and a compound (Chapter 1).

7. Recognize that atoms may join together to form molecules (Chapter 1).

8. Identify and interpret the chemical formulas of some simple compounds (Chapter 1).

9. Explain what a mixture is and cite examples to demonstrate this knowledge (Chapter 1).

10. Explain the differences between solutions and suspensions (Chapter 1).

11. Understand that compounds are categorized as either organic or inorganic (Chapter 1).

12. Recognize some common inorganic compounds and describe their uses (Chapter 1).

13. Identify the reasons why standard measurements are necessary (Chapter 1).

14. Know the units that are used to measure length, mass, temperature, and time (Chapter 1).

15. Use the appropriate tools to measure mass, volume, and temperature (Chapter 1).

    Measure volume, mass, and distance using metric units.

    Use a metric balance to measure mass.

    Use a graduated cylinder to measure volume.

    Use a metric rule to measure distance.

    Use and read a Celsius thermometer

16. Name the states of matter and cite their characteristics (Chapter 1).

17. Explain how the arrangement of particles affects the state of matter (Chapter 1).

18. Define the terms *liquid, solid,* and *gas* (Chapter 1).

19. List the names of approximately 30 elements along with their matching symbols, and recognize their properties and characteristics (Chapter 1).

20. Name the atomic particles that make up an element (Chapter 1).

21. Locate elements on a periodic chart (Chapter 1).

22. Name and locate the parts of an atom and cite their properties (Chapter 1).

23. Demonstrate how to use the periodic table to determine atomic mass/weight and atomic number (Chapter 1).

24. Compare and contrast models of the atom throughout history (Chapter 1).

25. Explain the differences among a compound, element, and mixture, and distinguish each (Chapter 1).

26. Separate a mixture into all of its components (Chapter 1).

27. Demonstrate that mixtures contain two or more elements that have not joined together, although they are in close contact (Chapter 1).

28. Explain that mixtures can be made up of two or more compounds (Chapter 2).

29. Explain that mixtures can be made up of several different elements and compounds (Chapter 2).

30. Explain that a mixture equals two or more materials that, when combined, each retains its original properties (Chapter 2).

31. Explain that mixtures can be solutions (Chapter 2).

32. Explain that a solution is one substance that is dissolved into another substance (Chapter 2).

33. Cite the common compound when given its formula, and vice versa (Chapter 1).

34. Describe a radioactive element (Chapters 1, 2).

35. Explain physical and chemical properties, differentiate between them, and cite examples of each (Chapters 1, 2).

36. Recognize that energy is required to change matter from one state to another (Chapter 2).

37. Explain the difference between nuclear fusion and nuclear fission (Chapter 2).

38. Explain chemical bonding (Chapter 2).

39. Differentiate between chemical and physical changes in matter (Chapter 2).

40. Define the law of conservation of matter (Chapter 2).

41. Name the four basic types of chemical reactions, citing examples of each (syntheses, single replacement, decomposition, double replacement) (Chapter 2).

42. Explain oxidation/valence and demonstrate how to determine it for common elements (Chapter 2).

43. Compare and contrast a chemical change and a physical change (Chapter 2).

44. Understand that a chemical change results in a change in chemical properties (Chapter 2).

Chapter 1
Mass and Measurement

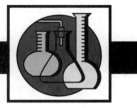

■ Teaching Resources

Books containing experiment(s) relating to the subject matter are marked with a plus sign (+) before and after the title.

P   *Capacity*, by Henry Pluckrose (Franklin Watts, 1995)
Full-page photographs and brief text describe capacity and how we measure it, connecting it to mathematics.

P   +*Length,*+ by Henry Pluckrose (Franklin Watts, 1995)
Combines mathematics and science to learn about measuring length and height, concentrating on predicting.

P   *Weight*, by Henry Pluckrose (Franklin Watts, 1995)
Makes the mathematics and science connection, in simplistic terms, about the many types and uses of weight.

P/I   +*Experiments with Heat,*+ by Walter Oleksy (Children's Press, 1986)
Simplistic text and accompanying experiments describe the nature of heat, its sources, movement, and effects on matter.

P/I   *How to Think Like a Scientist: Answering Questions by the Scientific Method,* by Stephen P. Kramer (HarperCollins, 1987)
This is a good introduction to the scientific method of investigation. Hypothetical situations are used as models.

I   +*Between Fire and Ice, the Science of Heat,*+ by Dr. David Darling (Dillon, 1992)
Informative text and accompanying experiments teach about heat and its effects.

I   +*It's a Gas!,*+ by Margaret Griffin and Ruth Griffin (Kids Can Press, 1993)
Facts and fun, with loads of activities, describe gases, their properties, and how they differ from liquids and solids; gases in our body; gases used for lighting, heating and refrigeration; and gases in our environment: oxygen, nitrogen, and carbon dioxide.

I   +*Solids and Liquids,*+ by David Glover (Kingfisher, 1993)
Describes the composition and strength of materials, both solid and liquid, and includes experiments and chemical reactions, through simplistic text and excellent illustrations.

I/U *Atoms and Cells,* by Lionel Bender (Gloucester Press, 1990)
Concise text, with good photographs, introduces the microscopic plant and animal life, viruses, microspores, and other life forms that can only be viewed with the aid of a microscope.

I/U +*From Glasses to Gases, the Science of Matter,*+ by Dr. David Darling (Dillon, 1992)
Explores matter and the forms it can take under different conditions, through helpful text and experiments.

I/U *Matter,* by Christopher Cooper (Dorling Kindersley, 1992)
Describes the elements that compose the physical world and matter's properties and behavior.

I/U *Structure of Matter* (Time-Life, 1992)
Describes, through a question-and-answer format, the structure and nature of matter and ways in which it can change.

U   *Force and Motion,* by Peter Lafferty (Dorling Kindersley, 1992)
Describes force and motion principles throughout history, including floating and sinking, Newton's and Galileo's principles, gravity, weight and mass, friction, and speed.

U +*Secrets of the Universe, Discovering the Universal Laws of Science,*+ by Paul Fleisher (Atheneum, 1987)
Details the laws of physics, such as planetary motion, Newton's laws of motion, gravity, the behavior of gases, and quantum mechanics.

■ Reading Selections

Books marked with an asterisk (*) before and after the title are related to activities in the activity sections of this chapter.

All Creatures Great and Small, by James Herriot (St. Martin's Press, 1992)
> Further adventures of the country veterinarian and the many animals he treats. (Chapter Book)

Awfully Short for the Fourth Grade, by Elvira Woodruff (Dell, 1995)
> When nine-year-old Noah's wish to become small comes true, the entire school is disrupted. (Chapter Book)

Big Bad Bruce, by Bill Peet (Houghton Mifflin, 1982)
> Bruce, a big bear, is a bully in the forest. Bruce picks on all the smaller creatures until the day he makes the mistake of bothering a little witch and her cat.

A Big Fat Enormous Lie, by Marjorie Weinman Sharmat (E. P. Dutton, 1993)
> After a little boy tells his mother and father a lie, he finds that it just keeps getting bigger and bigger until he tells the truth.

The Biggest House in the World, by Leo Lionni (Alfred A. Knopf, 1987)
> When a little snail wishes for the biggest house in the world, his father tells him a story to show why this would not be wise.

The Biggest Nose, by Kathy Caple (Houghton Mifflin, 1988)
> Eleanor, the elephant, attempts to be like everyone else after she is teased about having the biggest nose. She finally realizes that everyone has some feature that is more prominent than the others.

The Bite of the Gold Bug, by Barthe DeClements (Puffin Books, 1994)
> Bucky and his father must overcome many dangerous obstacles while mining for gold in Alaska. (Chapter Book)

Buford the Little Bighorn, by Bill Peet (Houghton Mifflin, 1983)
> Buford's huge horns made it unsafe for him to be climbing around the mountains like his friends. He was very unhappy until he realized that he could put his horns to good use.

The Country Bunny and the Little Gold Shoes, by Dubose Heyward (Houghton Mifflin, 1974)
> A country bunny is named the Easter Bunny, despite being the mother of 21 children, when cleverness and kindness win out over size and muscle.

George Shrinks, by William Joyce (HarperCollins Juvenile Books, 1998)
> George tries to take care of the cat and his baby brother even though he awakes to find that he is the size of a mouse.

The Giant Jam Sandwich, by John Vernon Lord (Houghton Mifflin, 1987)
> To catch a huge swarm of wasps, a town constructs the biggest jam sandwich ever.

The Great Quillow, by James Thurber (Harcourt Brace, 1994)
> A tiny toy maker defeats a giant and saves his town. (Chapter Book)

Gulliver's Travels, by Jonathan Swift (Oxford University Press Children's Books, 1994)
> An Englishman travels to a land of people six inches tall, a land of giants, and an island of sorcerers. (Chapter Book)

How Big Is a Foot?, by Rolf Myller (Young Yearling, 1991)
> When the king uses his foot to measure a bed for the queen, he learns that everyone's method of measurement is not the same and that there is a need for a form of standard measurement.

Hue Boy, by Rita Phillips Mitchell (Penguin, 1999)
> Although everyone in his village gives him helpful advice, Hue Boy does not grow. He learns, however, that there are several ways to "stand tall."

In the Haunted House, by Eve Bunting (Houghton Mifflin, 1994)
> The illustrations show two pairs of sneakers, one big and one small, as a little girl and her father tour a dark, old house.

Inch by Inch, by Leo Lionni (Mulberry Books, 1995)
> The little inchworm agrees to measure the parts of many different birds in an attempt to keep from being eaten.

Jamaica Tag-Along, by Juanita Havill (Houghton Mifflin, 1989)
> Jamaica doesn't want a younger child hanging around until she remembers how it felt when her brother treated her the same way.

Jethro and Joel Were a Troll, by Bill Peet (Houghton Mifflin, 1990)
> Jethro, part of a giant, two-headed troll, tries to save the countryside from Joel's rampage.

Little Gorilla, by Ruth Bornstein (Houghton Mifflin, 1986)
> A rhythmic text tells of Little Gorilla, whom everyone in the jungle loved, even when he kept growing, and growing, and growing.

Little Tricker the Squirrel Meets Big Double the Bear, by Ken Kesey (Puffin Books, 1992)
   Little Tricker gets revenge on Big Double after watching him terrorize the forest animals.

Moon Tiger, by Phyllis Root (Grove Press, 1997)
   When Jessica Ellen gets in trouble because of her little brother, she dreams of a huge tiger who could come and, possibly, eat her little brother.

"No!" Said Joe, by John Prater (Candlewick Press, 1996)
   When Joe continues to be uncooperative, his parents threaten several punishments, including leaving him with a giant.

Nora and the Great Bear, by Ute Krause (Penguin, 1992)
   After Nora learns to hunt, she dreams of capturing the Great Bear of the forest. Her desires change, however, after she becomes lost in the forest.

St. Patrick's Day in the Morning, by Eve Bunting (Ticknor & Fields, 1983)
   A little boy wishes to find a way to prove that he is not too small to march in the St. Patrick's Day parade.

Teeny Tiny, by Jill Bennett (Paper Star, 1998)
   Tells the tale of a teeny-tiny woman who finds a teeny-tiny bone in a churchyard.

Treasure in the Stream, by Dorothy Hoobler (Silver Burdett, 1991)
   Ten-year-old Amy and her family find their lives changed forever when gold is discovered in California. (Chapter Book)

Windows of Gold and Other Golden Tales, by Selma Lanes (Simon & Schuster, 1989)
   Stories from around the world tell how gold can make dreams come true or ruin fortunes. (Chapter Book)

You're a Little Kid with a Big Heart, by Bernard Waber (Houghton Mifflin, 1980)
   Octavia decides she would rather remain a little girl after being given her wish to be a grown-up.

The following books are out of print, but may be available at the local library.

Big and Little, by Ruth Krauss (Scholastic, 1987)
   Text and illustrations help describe some of the little things that big things love.

Big, Small, Short, Tall, by Loreen Leedy (Holiday House, 1987)
   Performing animals present 13 pairs of opposites like: big-small and short-tall.

The Biggest, Meanest, Ugliest Dog in the Whole Wide World, by Rebecca C. Jones (Macmillan, 1982)
   Jonathan is frightened of the dog next door, until an accident changes their relationship.

Do I Have to Take Violet?, by Sucie Stevenson (G. P. Putnam's Sons, 1987)
   Ely at first is not happy about having to take her little sister to play by the sea.

Farmer Mack Measures His Pig, by Tony Johnston (Harper & Row, 1986)
   Chaos reigns on Farmer Mack's farm when he attempts to measure his fat pig.

Fletcher and the Great Big Dog, by Jane Kopper Hilleary (Houghton Mifflin, 1988)
   Fletcher tries to run away from a big dog that scares him only to be glad the dog is around when Fletcher finds himself lost.

Friska, the Sheep That was Too Small, by Rob Lewis (Farrar, Straus & Giroux, 1988)
> The other sheep made fun of Friska because she was so small, until she showed them that being small has its advantages.

Gobs of Goo, by Vicki Cobb (HarperCollins, 1983)
> Several types of sticky substances are described, plus how they are made and used.

Molly Pink Goes Hiking, by Judith Caseley (Greenwillow Books, 1985)
> Molly learns not to judge people by their size when she goes hiking with her family.

New House, by Joyce Maynard (Harcourt Brace Jovanovich, 1987)
> Andy is taught to measure and plan when he builds a treehouse out of scrap material from a nearby building site.

Smaller Than Most, by Shirley Lincoln Rigby (Harper & Row, 1985)
> Three short stories that show how Won-Ton's family is growing and, although he is smaller than most of his friends, good things do come in small packages.

Soup for Supper, by Phyllis Root (Harper & Row, 1986)
> A wee little woman and a giant find that they can share vegetable soup and an unlikely friendship.

The Story of Imelda, Who Was Small, by Morris Lurie (Houghton Mifflin, 1988)
> Imelda's family sets out to discover why she is so small.

■ Science Activities

Volume and Density

Use pasta to demonstrate volume and density to the class. Measure 1 cup of uncooked pasta and weigh it. Prepare the pasta according to the package instructions. Have a student measure the pasta again. Ask the class: How many cups of pasta do you have now? What does all the pasta weigh? What does one cup of the cooked pasta weigh? Which is denser, cooked pasta or uncooked pasta? Why?

Density 1

Have students help with this demonstration of measuring density. Cut several different items into the same size (approximately 1 by 1 by 1/2 inch). You could use such things as bread, an apple, a potato, wood, Styrofoam, or watermelon. Have a different student weigh each sample, then ask the class if the samples weigh the same. (Some samples have more mass with the same volume.) Repeat the process with different liquids, such as water, oil, corn syrup, and catsup. Do the liquids differ in weight? (Again, some samples have more mass with the same volume.) What you are comparing is the density of these items, or the mass in a certain volume of matter (mass divided by volume).

Density 2

Following is another demonstration of density that students can assist with:

- Ask a student to pour 1/4 cup of corn syrup into a tall, narrow, clear glass, graduated cylinder, or clear plastic container (or add smaller amounts to a test tube). Allow time for all the syrup to run to the bottom of the container. Then have another student add 1/4 cup of water that has been tinted with blue food coloring. Next, ask a third student to add 1/4 cup of vegetable oil. Finally, have a fourth student add 1/4 cup of rubbing alcohol that has been tinted with red food coloring. Ask the class: What happens to the liquids in the container? Why? (The liquids form layers because they have different densities.) What other properties of the liquids could be different? (Their boiling points and freezing points.)

- Ask another student to drop several objects into the container. (Lightweight objects such as Styrofoam, a piece of hard-cooked egg white, a plastic bead, a rubber band, a toothpick, or a piece of celery work best.) Ask the class: Where do the objects come to rest? How can density be used to characterize solids?
- Stir the liquids and observe them again the next day. Ask the students to describe what happens.

Volume

Explain to students that volume can be defined as the amount of space an object takes up, then use the following activity to demonstrate measuring volume:

- Bring in a box of sugar cubes and a small, empty box. Tell the students that each cube is approximately 1 centimeter high, 1 centimeter wide, and 1 centimeter thick. This cube is one "cubic centimeter."
- Fill the box with sugar cubes. Have the students count how many cubes fill the box. That number is the volume in cubic centimeters.

Measuring Fluids

- Ask the class if they have ever heard a doctor order 10 cc's of a fluid. Explain to them that "cc" represents "cubic centimeter," which is used to measure volume. Another name for a cubic centimeter is a milliliter (ml). Fluids and liquids are often measured in milliliters.
- Ask students if they know how many milliliters are in one liter (milli = 1,000) and how many milliliters are in a two-liter bottle of soda (2,000).
- If possible, show the class a graduated cylinder and point out the marked-off units. Measure 1/4 cup of water and pour it into the cylinder. Ask the students: How many milliliters is it? What is the metric volume of 1/4 cup of liquid? Repeat this procedure with other amounts of liquid.

More on Density

- To perform this experiment, you will need several cans of different types of soda (you must have at least one diet soda and one regular soda) and a large bucket or tank of water (a small aquarium-style tank works well for visual effect).
- Before starting the actual experiment, have the students predict what will happen when you try to float the different cans of soda in the tank of water. Record their predictions.
- Place the unopened cans, one at a time, in the tank of water and record what happens (the diet soda will float; the regular soda will sink). Discuss possible reasons for what happens and record the class's explanations.
- With a scale or balance, find the mass of each can. (Diet soda will have a mass of 10–15 grams less than regular soda.) Ask the students to look at the order of ingredients listed on the cans and see how they compare.
- Further explore by changing the water temperature. (Warm water is less dense, so diet sodas are more likely to sink.)

Weight

Explain to the class that to measure the amount of mass an object has on Earth, you can use a scale to determine its weight, and a specific type of equipment that is used for determining mass is a balance. Obtain a balance, if possible, one for every two or three students in the class. You may be able to borrow one or more balances from your local junior high or high school. There are also some balances for sale that are relatively inexpensive. Use the balance(s) to compare masses of a number of everyday items. This is also an excellent way to familiarize students with the metric system. (A paper clip weighs about 1 gram. A two-liter bottle of soda weights approximately 2,000 grams.) Weigh several items and have the students determine the metric weight and the conventional English/American weight for the items.

Property

Explain to the class that a "property" is something that characterizes or describes matter. On individual index cards, place the names of different objects, one per card (e.g., apple, milk, cotton, hot chocolate, marble, nail, air, water, toothpick, rubber band). Ask the students to identify all the objects that are 1) red, 2) liquid, 3) stretchy, 4) hot, 5) made of wood, or 6) heavy. Have them determine what properties they have identified (red = color; liquids = physical state; stretchy = elasticity; hot = temperature; made of wood = composition; heavy = density/weight). Have students come up with more properties to identify (e.g., volume, size).

Length

- Show the students a yardstick or meterstick, a ruler (preferably with both inches and centimeters), and a tape measure (both the type commonly used by carpenters and the type commonly used by seamstresses). Ask the class why they think we need so many different measuring devices, and when and why it is important to know the length or width of an object.

- Using the measuring tools you have gathered, have the students measure a variety of objects, such as a book, their thumbs, a pencil, a desk, a door, a poster, and a person's height. Discuss again why so many different measuring tools are used and why measurement is important.

- Have the students brainstorm different ways they could measure the circumference of a ball. Then show them how you can wrap a piece of string around the object and then lay the string on a ruler or yardstick/meterstick to find the length around the ball.

- Measure the object again with a measuring tape. Did you get the same measurement? Ask the students in what situations it would be easier to use a tape measure than a ruler. Have students practice using a tape measure by measuring their wrists, their heads, and their waists. (*Farmer Mack Measures His Pig* by Johnston)

- Give each child a straw cut to the length of his or her foot to serve as a personal measuring unit. Have the students measure different objects to see how many of their units are required. (Have them predict how many units the object is before they measure.) Ask them to look for objects that are exactly the same size as their measuring unit.

- Borrow a device used in shoe stores to measure shoe size. Chart and graph each child's foot size. Older students can predict, then prove, whether there is any relationship between height and foot length.

Make Your Own Goo

Following the directions in *Gobs of Goo* by Cobb, have the class make several different varieties of "goo." Examine the end result of each recipe and record the properties of each. Make a class chart comparing the properties of the different varieties of goo.

Which One Goes Where?

Obtain a number of different items that will fit inside one another. Ask the students to predict the order in which they fit together by sight only. Test the students' hypotheses to see if they are correct. Do the objects fit together in more than one way?

Step By Step

Compare approximately how many steps a person would take to cover a specific distance to the steps that would be taken by different-sized animals. Have students predict what the results will be and then obtain books from the library on the different animals to determine what the length of each animal's stride is.

On Your Mark, Get Set, Go!

Mark an area outside of your school or home to run races on. Have the students measure specific distances for different races and use chalk, string, rope, or ribbon to mark the track for each race. Then have the students run races so that they can determine which distances they are best at running, hopping, skipping, and so forth.

Chromatography

Explain to the students that chromatography is a process used to separate a substance into its components. The process is based on the principle that different substances have different densities. Demonstrate this process in action using the following activity:

- Cut a long strip (about 2 inches wide) out of a coffee filter. Tape one end of the strip to the middle of a pencil so that the strip hangs down from the pencil.
- Lay the pencil across a glass and cut the length of the strip so that the strip almost touches the bottom of the glass. Lift out the strip and place a dab of black ink on it (about 1 to 2 inches from the bottom). (Do not use permanent markers!) Add some water to the glass so that the water level is about 1/2 inch.
- Lower the strip into the water and rest the pencil across the glass. Ask the students to describe what they see as the water rises. You will be able to see the ink separate into the different colors that make up the black color. (The different colors have different densities.)
- Try other liquids and observe the different bands of colors it produces. (Advanced students can research some of the applications for chromatography.)

Icicles

After a cold spell, take the class outside to measure and compare icicles. Ask them to determine if there is any correlation between length and where the icicles were found.

Positive and Negative Charges

- To demonstrate that atoms have positive and negative charges, cut out 15 to 20 small circles with a paper punch. Scatter the circles on a table. Inflate a balloon, rub it across your hair several times, and then hold it close to, but not touching, the paper circles. The paper will "jump" up and attach itself to the balloon.
- Explain to the class that all matter, paper in this case, is made up of atoms. Each atom has a positive center with negative-charged electrons around it. The balloon rubs the electrons off

the hair, giving the balloon extra negative charges. The positive part of the paper circle is attracted to the extra negative charge on the balloon that allows the paper to overcome the forces of gravity.

Atoms and Electricity

- Explain to the students that the atom is composed of three types of particles: protons, neutrons, and electrons. The electrons orbit around the other two, which combine to form the nucleus of the atom. When these electrons flow from atom to atom in a loop or circuit, electricity is formed.

- Have the class research different types of circuits to determine the path electrons must flow to complete the loop. They should note that if the circuit is broken in any part of the loop, the electrons stop flowing, and no electricity is produced. (See Section 1, Chapter 1, "Magnets and Electricity," for additional activities on electricity.)

Let's Build an Atom

- Tell the class that even the ancient Greeks believed that everything was made up of tiny, invisible particles, which they classified into four elements: fire, water, air, and earth. Today we believe that all matter is made of electrically charged particles (electrons, protons, and neutrons) that group together to form more than 100 elements.

- Have the students research the structure of an atom and the different combinations of electrons, protons, and neutrons in each element.

- To help them visualize the components of an atom, have them cut out twenty 2-inch circles of red construction paper, twenty 2-inch circles of green construction paper, and twenty-two 1/2-inch circles of yellow construction paper. (Other colors may be substituted.) Magnetic marbles work great for this activity, too. Tell the students to write "P+" on each of the red circles, "N" on the green circles, and "E-" on the small yellow circles. These represent protons, neutrons, and electrons and their charges. Have the students place two red circles and two green circles in the center of a round plate and two yellow circles on the rim of the plate. Explain to them that the center pile is the "nucleus" of the atom and the electrons are orbiting around the nucleus. The charge of the atom is zero. (The two + charges in the nucleus "cancel" the two - charges of the orbiting electrons.) This represents a helium atom.

- To determine the "atomic number" of an atom, have the students count the number of protons in the nucleus. (The atomic number of helium is 2.) To determine the "atomic mass" of an atom, have them count the number of protons plus neutrons in the nucleus. (The atomic mass of helium is 4.) Point out that the electrons are so light and moving so rapidly that they are not part of the atomic mass.

- Ask the students to create some other atoms and determine their atomic number and atomic mass, using the information in the following chart.

	In the Center of the Plate, Place		Along the Rim, Place	Element
Red Circles	Green Circles		Yellow Circles	
1	0		1	hydrogen
3	4		3	lithium
5	6		5	boron
6	6		6	carbon
7	7		7	nitrogen
8	8		8	oxygen
9	10		9	fluorine
10	10		10	neon
11	12		11	sodium
17	18		17	chlorine

Have the students identify the atomic number and the atomic mass of each element. (hydrogen AN = 1, AM = 1; lithium AN = 3, AM = 7; boron AN = 5, AM = 11; carbon AN = 6, AM = 12; nitrogen AN = 7, AM = 14; oxygen AN = 8, AM = 16; fluorine AN = 9, AM = 19; neon AN = 10, AM = 20; sodium AN = 11, AM = 23; chlorine AN = 17, AM = 35.)

- Show the class a periodic table of elements. Can they determine what some of the numbers represent?

The Bigger Bubble Bottle Battle

- Have the students predict which soda product contains the most bubbles (carbonation), then perform this experiment to see if their predictions were correct. To do the experiment, you will need several same-sized bottles of cold, carbonated drinks (ginger-ale, cola, and club soda will all work) and the same number of identical-sized balloons. Have two students do the experiment. Take the labels off the bottles so that the class will have a better view of what is happening.

- While one person holds a bottle by its mouth, the other person should remove the cap from the bottle and, very quickly, stretch one of the balloons over the mouth of the bottle.

- Watch how big the balloon gets. Ask the class to guess what is causing the balloon to expand. What happens if the student gently shakes or squeezes the bottle?

- Have a new pair of students repeat this process with each bottle of soda. Record the results of each experiment. When the experiments are completed, rank the bottles according to balloon size.

- Explain to the class that the bubbles in soda products are a gas called carbon dioxide. The gas is forced into the bottle under extreme pressure at the bottling plant. Then the bottle is quickly capped. When we buy the soda and uncap the bottle, the pressure is released, which forces the gas out of the bottle. Putting a balloon over the top of the mouth of the bottle traps the gas that stretches the balloon as the gas is released from the bottle. The more gas, the bigger the balloon. If we try to squeeze the balloon to force the gas back into the bottle, it won't stay because we can't use as much pressure as the factory did when the soda was originally bottled.

A Shell-Less Egg

As a demonstration, place an egg in a cup of acetic acid (vinegar). Let the egg sit in the vinegar for two or three days. Ask the class if they can explain what happens. (The acid reacts with the eggshell, but not with the egg membrane, and forms a shell-less egg.)

Where Did the Sugar Go?

Demonstrate evaporation using the following experiment:

- In a test tube or saucepan, make a solution of sugar and water (one part sugar to four parts water). Do not get any of the solution on the sides of the test tube or pan.
- Heat the test tube over a candle or place a lid on the saucepan and heat at medium low heat. Heat the solution until you see condensation on the sides of the test tube or on the lid of the pan.
- Have students taste this liquid. Is it sweet? Can they explain why or why not? (Only the water molecules evaporate, leaving the sugar molecules behind in the test tube or pan.)

Mixtures

- Explain to students that a "mixture" can be said to be the combination of at least two substances that, when thoroughly mixed, still retain their own individual properties. The population of the United States is a mixture of races, a baseball team has a mixture of positions, a salad is a mixture of vegetables. Make a class list of five mixtures and the substances that make them up.
- Demonstrate examples of mixtures by 1) combining cinnamon and sugar; 2) combining oil and vinegar; and 3) adding several objects (paper clips, marbles, toothpicks) to a glass of water. Point out that, even when thoroughly mixed, the ingredients retain their own existence. (You can see specks of sugar and specks of cinnamon, the oil and water separate, and the objects are still visible in the water.)
- Ask students to separate a mixture of sand and salt. First, mix together one part sand and one part salt (or use sugar). Give a portion of the mixture (1/4 to 1/2 cup) to each student. (Using a zipping storage bag works well.) Challenge each student to find a way to separate the sand from the salt. (Be prepared for a "that's impossible" reaction.) The students may discover that, when water is added, the salt dissolves and the sand settles to the bottom. (The salt and water form a solution.) The salt could then be reduced to a solid state by boiling the solution until the water is gone and only the salt crystals remain.
- *Challenge:* Ask students to figure out how to separate a mixture of iron filings and sand. (Use a magnet.)

Molecules

All substances are made of small particles called molecules. Demonstrate how a mixture of molecules can be divided while still retaining the properties of the original molecule by doing one or more of the following experiments:

- Drop several coffee crystals into warm water and have students record their observations immediately, then again after two or three hours.
- Place a drop of food coloring in a container of water. Ask students to describe what happens.
- Place a mothball, or solid air freshener, in the room. Notice the smell. (These are molecules escaping into the air that your nose can detect.) After two or three weeks, observe the mothball or freshener again. Ask the students to describe what has happened to it and explain why. (The

objects become smaller and smaller, even to the point that they cannot be seen individually, but still continue to exist.)

Molecules and Compounds

- Explain to the class that molecules are groups of atoms. Some molecules may simply be two atoms of the same element, such as O_2, an oxygen molecule consisting of two oxygen atoms. Others combine different elements. H_2O is a water molecule consisting of two hydrogen atoms and one oxygen atom. NaCl (sodium chloride, or table salt) has one atom of sodium (Na) and one atom of chlorine (Cl). When two or more types of elements combine, a "compound" has been created.

- Have the students create compounds by using gumdrops and toothpicks. Assign an element to each color of gumdrop (white = carbon, orange = hydrogen, green = oxygen, etc.). Explain to the students that each color gumdrop must have a different number of toothpicks stuck in it. (Hydrogen can have only one toothpick inserted; oxygen must have two; carbon must have four, etc.) Ask the students to create compounds such as CO_2, CH_4, and H_2O.

- Students will quickly find that there is only one formation for each compound that meets the toothpick requirements. With older students, you can explain that the number of toothpicks is related to the number of electrons an atom releases or gains.

Reactions!

- Explain to the students that the number of atoms that combine to form a compound depends upon the charge of an ion. For example, oxygen ions have a charge of –2. Hydrogen ions have a charge of +1. Therefore, to have an uncharged, stable molecule of water, two hydrogen ions combine with one oxygen ion to form the water molecule H_2O. This reaction can be written as an equation: $2 H^+ + O^{-2} = H_2O$. The reaction of forming table salt would be: $Na^{+1} + Cl^{-1} = NaCl$. Sometimes, compounds can have charges, too and react: (OH = -1, NH_4 = +1); $K^{+1} + (OH)^{-1} = KOH$; $(NH_4)^{+1} = (OH)^{-1} = NH_4OH$.

- Ask the students what the following reactions would produce. Remind them that the number of atoms must be the same on both sides of the equation.

  $H^+ + Cl^- =$

  $Al^{+3} + Br^{-1} =$

  $Ag^+ + Cl^- =$

  $Zn^{+2} + O^{-2} =$

  $(NH_4)+ + Cl^- =$

  (Answers: HCl, $AlBr_3$, AgCl, ZnO, NH_4Cl.) Again, remind the students that the number of atoms must be the same, and the charge must be zero. It would take three Br ions to bond with one Al+3 ions, producing $AlBr_3$.

Easy Come, Easy Go!

Give the class the following information about atoms:

Sometimes atoms gain or lose electrons. If an atom loses one electron, there is then one more proton than electrons, so the atom has a charge of +1. If two electrons are lost, the charge becomes +2. Similarly, if one electron is gained, there are more electrons than protons, and the charge becomes -1. These charged atoms are called ions. Because opposites attract, two oppositely charged ions are attracted to each other (the basis for chemical reactions).

Occasionally, a nucleus can vary in the number of neutrons. The number of protons ALWAYS remains the same for each element. For example, a uranium atom always has 92 protons. However, some uranium atoms have 143 neutrons (92 protons + 143 neutrons = 235) and are called U-235. Other uranium atoms have 146 neutrons (3 extra) and are called U-238. Atoms that contain the same number of protons, but different numbers of neutrons, are called *isotopes*. Isotopes of an element have the same chemical properties, but may have different nuclear properties (because their nuclei are different). Some unstable isotopes can emit particles and emit energy rays. This is called *radiation*. As the isotopes emit radiation and try to become more stable, it is said that the isotopes are undergoing "radioactive decay."

Have the students research the Curies and their work, looking for answers to the following questions: What elements were they working with? What discoveries did they make? Were there any side effects resulting from their work?

Solution or Suspension: "DRINK UP!"

Ask the students to do these experiments at home and answer the questions.

- Make a glass or pitcher of sweetened iced tea. (Use instant tea.) What happens to the sugar and tea particles? You've created a solution. What ingredient is the solvent? (The water.) What ingredients are solutes? (sugar and tea.) Once mixed, does the solution stay mixed?

- Make a glass of chocolate milk by adding chocolate syrup to milk. Add enough chocolate so that some settles to the bottom. Why didn't it stay mixed? (It's a suspension.)

- Other solutions include powdered lemonade, limeade, and fruit punch. Other suspensions include orange juice or fresh lemonade (where the particles can settle).

Everyday Chemistry

Tell the students that the following compounds are household products, or are easily available at a hardware store. Ask them to find the common name for each compound and determine how many atoms of each element are in each molecule. They can use a periodic chart of elements to find the names of the elements.

1. NH_4OH (ammonium hydroxide)

2. $CaCO_3$ (calcium carbonate)

3. $CaSO_4$ (calcium sulfate)

4. $C_6H_{12}O_6$ (glucose)

5. $MgSO_4$ (magnesium sulfate)

6. $NaHCO_3$ (sodium bicarbonate)

7. $C_{12}H_{22}O_{11}$ (sucrose)

8. $NaClO_{11}$ (sodium hypochlorite)

Answers:

1. household ammonia—1 nitrogen, 5 hydrogen, 1 oxygen

2. lime—1 calcium, 1 carbon, 3 oxygen

3. plaster of Paris—1 calcium, 1 sulfur, 4 oxygen

4. corn syrup—6 carbon, 12 hydrogen, 6 oxygen

5. epsom salts—1 magnesium, 1 sulfur, 4 oxygen

6. baking soda—1 sodium, 1 hydrogen, 1 carbon, 3 oxygen

7. sugar—12 carbon, 22 hydrogen, 11 oxygen

8. bleach—1 sodium, 1 chlorine, 1 oxygen

Solvents and Solutions

Do the following experiment to demonstrate solvents and solutions:

- Fill four test tubes, or small jars, one-third full with water (room temperature). Add 1/4 teaspoon of table salt to test tube #1. Shake vigorously until the salt is dissolved. Continue to add salt, in 1/4-teaspoon increments, until no more will dissolve and some salt settles to the bottom of the tube. Record how much salt was added to reach this point of saturation.

- Repeat the process with tubes #2, #3, and #4, using sugar, baking soda, and epsom salts, respectively. Explain to the class that the water is the solvent in which the materials are dissolved. The molecules are not reacting with the water, they are just being dispersed throughout the liquid. (To prove this point, see the "Solutions" activity in Chapter 2 in this section, in which salt is dissolved and then recovered.)

- Heat the test tubes over a flame, or heat the jars by placing them either in a microwave oven or a saucepan of hot water. Stir the solutions. Ask a student to record whether heating the solution caused more of the material to dissolve. Ask the class how this knowledge could be important.

- Another good way to demonstrate the formation of a saturated solution is to prepare a recipe of fudge or candy. (The old-fashioned way, using a candy thermometer and lots of boiling.) Can the students explain why it is important to boil the mixture so long?

Is Your Water Acidic or Basic?

Explain to the class that some substances become very reactive in water. How they react characterizes them as acids or bases. To demonstrate how acids and bases can react, visit the produce department of your supermarket.

- Purchase a small amount of broccoli, red cabbage, carrots, and onions. In class, divide each vegetable into three portions. Place one portion of each vegetable in a saucepan with one cup of water (preferably de-ionized) and bring it to a boil. After three minutes, cover the saucepan and cook for five additional minutes. Remove the broccoli, red cabbage, and onions. Replace the cover and cook the carrots for seven additional minutes. Place all four cooked vegetables on a plate and label it "water."

- Repeat the cooking process with the second portion of vegetables. This time, add 1/2 teaspoon of baking soda to the water before adding the vegetables. Cook in the same manner as above. Place these vegetables on a plate labeled "basic."

- For the third group, add one teaspoon of vinegar to the water before adding the vegetables. Cook as described above, then place on a plate labeled "acidic."

- Have the students to compare the color, texture, and flavor of each group. Ask them: Did some pigments react favorably with acids while others reacted favorably with bases? Would you expect most "tap" water to be acidic or basic? (Most tap water is slightly basic due to the lime/limestone underground.)

■ Creative Writing Activities

Following are instructions to give the students for various writing activities.

- Discuss with your class the phrase "larger than life" and its meaning. Think of some people (fictitious and real) who fit this description. (Some examples are George Washington, Benjamin Franklin, John Henry, Thomas Edison, Paul Bunyan, Sluefoot Sue, and Superman.) Write your own story about a person, real or imaginary, whom you consider larger than life.

- Write a history of how your family has grown over the years. Start with the marriage of your parents and include the arrival of children (including yourself). Draw a family tree to go along with your history. The family tree can include grandparents, aunts, uncles, and cousins, too. (*Smaller Than Most* by Rigby)

- Write a story with a plot that centers around a problem that can only be solved by someone (or something) who is small in stature. (*Friska, the Sheep That Was Too Small* by Lewis)

- People often think that "bigger is better." We want the biggest house and the biggest piece of cake. We think being the tallest and the oldest makes us the best. However, there is a saying that "good things come in small packages." Explain what you think this saying means and list as many examples, with explanations, as you can. (*Big and Little* by Krauss)

- A small Western town suddenly becomes a boom town due to the discovery of gold in the hills nearby. Write a character study of a person who lived in the town prior to the gold discovery, describing how the event affects his or her daily life and personality.

- Write a story in which a smaller but more clever adversary outwits a bully. (*Little Tricker the Squirrel Meets Big Double the Bear* by Kesey; *Big Bad Bruce* by Peet)

- Write a silly tale in which the main character eats or drinks something that makes him or her shrink in size. You can do the same activity having the character grow or change into another form.

- Have you ever been in the situation of being an older brother/sister required to include a younger sibling in your plans for the day? (Or perhaps you were the younger sibling.) Write a story (from either perspective) of how the day went. Was it as bad (or good) as you anticipated? (*Do I Have to Take Violet?* by Stevenson; *Jamaica Tag-Along* by Havill)

- Write a story about an unlikely friendship between a very tiny creature and a very large creature. (*Soup for Supper* by Root)

- Pretend that you are very small and in an unusual setting, such as a fly in a zoo, a mouse on a pirate ship, or a bee at a honey festival. Write a story about your adventures. (*George Shrinks* by Joyce)

- You awake one morning to find that, although you are still the same size, you have become "lighter than air." How would your life change? Write a story from this new perspective.

- Think about your favorite drink. Does it come as a solid (must add water) or a liquid? Write a description of your drink, how it is made, its cost, and how it is stored. Come up with a poster to advertise this drink to your friends, convincing them that it is the only drink they should be drinking.

■ Art Activities

Following are instructions to give the students for various art activities.

- Make a blueprint for a tree house or backyard cottage that you would like to build. Make sure that your blueprint is done to scale. Make notations on the blueprint of what items you will use to decorate your new playhouse. (*New House* by Maynard)

- On the bottom of a white paper plate, draw a picture of a dog's face looking mean and scary. On the bottom of another plate, draw the same dog looking friendly and playful. Place the two plates on top of each other, blank sides together, and staple the plates to each other around the edges. You can staple an ice cream stick between the two plates sticking out from the bottom to serve as a handle. Cut pieces of yarn or construction paper in varying lengths and glue them to the edge of the paper plate to serve as hair for both dogs. Cut ears out of construction paper and staple them in place. Make up a story in which your dog changes from a good mood to a bad mood often, turning the plate to show the correct image of the dog as the story progresses. (*The Biggest, Meanest, Ugliest Dog in the Whole Wide World* by Jones; *Fletcher and the Great Big Dog* by Hilleary)

- Make a picture story cube that shows the chaos that results when a farmer attempts to measure his prize pig, bull, or other animal before entering it in the county fair. The premise of your picture story is that the animal is not willing to cooperate with the farmer as he tries to take the measurements he needs. (*Farmer Mack Measures His Pig* by Johnston) Draw each picture of your story on one of six 6-inch squares that you have cut out of poster board. When the drawings are complete, lay pictures one through four next to each other with their edges touching. Use colored tape to connect the four drawings to each other on the right side of the picture. Join the right edge of picture four to the left edge of picture one and tape them together. Then tape picture five to the top of your cube, and picture six to the bottom.

- Draw lines to divide a plain piece of white paper into four squares. In each square, draw pictures to demonstrate opposites, such as big-small, short-tall. (*Big, Small, Short, Tall* by Leedy)

- Make a picture in which as many objects as possible are made of geometric shapes of varying sizes (e.g., a snowman made of three different-sized circles, skyscrapers of different-sized rectangles, pyramids of triangles of varying sizes).

- Place a large piece of paper on the floor. You may want to put a piece of plastic under the paper to protect the carpet/flooring. Remove one sock and shoe and place your foot in a pan of water-based paint that you have placed next to the paper. There will be several pans, with a different-colored paint in each pan, for other students to use. Remove your foot from the paint, press it onto a spot on the paper, and write your name under the footprint. After all students have completed this process, and the paint has dried on the paper, your teacher will measure the different footprints to find the biggest, smallest, widest, narrowest, and so forth. (*How Big Is a Foot?* by Myller)

- Make abstract art pictures using all lines of one length, such as 2 inches, 4 inches, or 6 inches, or use the side of a piece of paper, the side of a box, a pencil, a straw, or an eraser to determine the length of your lines. How many different shapes can you make using only one line length?

- Make life-sized animal paw print stencils by tracing the prints on heavy cardboard and then cutting them out. Draw and identify each of the prints on chart paper, comparing their sizes. You can also make plaster of Paris molds of various prints by finding objects that can be pressed into the wet plaster to give the image of the pawprint. Use the dried molds as paperweights by gluing felt to the bottom of each.

- Fill several different containers with water. Color each container of water a different color using food coloring. Using coffee filters, dip areas of the filter in different bowls and watch the colors spread. Use several different filters and see how many different designs you can make. Then try dipping different types of paper (napkins, paper towels, grocery bags, construction paper, etc.) into the water. You will see that the heavier (denser) the paper is, the slower the colored water spreads across the sheet (the slower the absorption rate). Use the papers that color well for backgrounds for drawings. Each coffee filter can be gathered in the middle and attached to a clothespin with a pipe cleaner to make a butterfly.

Chapter 2
Physical and Chemical Changes

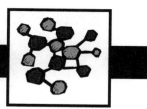

■ Teaching Resources

Books containing experiment(s) relating to the subject matter are marked with a plus sign (+) before and after the title.

I/U *Eyewitness Books: Chemistry,* by Ann Newmark (Dorling Kindersley, 1999)
Chemical reactions and the role of chemistry in our world are described through the help of close-up photographs.

■ Reading Selections

Books marked with an asterisk (*) before and after the title are related to activities in the activity sections of this chapter.

The Adventures of King Midas, by Lynne Reid Banks (Morrow Junior Books, 1992)
> King Midas regrets his wish that everything he touches should turn to gold and faces many tests to try to undo it. (Chapter Book)

Alice in Wonderland, by Lewis Carroll (Salem House, 1990)
> Describes Alice's adventures in Wonderland and the extraordinary comings and goings there. (Chapter Book)

Alphabet Soup, by Kate Banks (Alfred A. Knopf, 1994)
> A young boy takes a magical journey while spelling out words with his alphabet soup.

Arthur's April Fool, by Marc Brown (Little, Brown, 1985)
> Arthur experiences trouble with his magic tricks for the April Fool's Day school assembly.

Arthur's Nose, by Marc Brown (Little, Brown, 1986)
> Arthur visits a rhinologist when he is unhappy with the size of his nose.

Attaboy, Sam!, by Lois Lowry (Houghton Mifflin, 1992)
> Anastasia's little brother concocts a perfume from his mother's favorite smells as a home-made gift for her birthday. (Chapter Book)

Babushka's Doll, by Patricia Polacco (Simon & Schuster, 1994)
> When her grandmother's doll comes to life while Natasha is playing with it, she understands why Babushka played with the doll only once.

Bartholomew and the Oobleck, by Dr. Seuss (Random Library, 1987)
> The king asks the magician for something new to come out of the sky (rather than rain, snow, etc.). Oobleck becomes more than the king bargained for.

Big Anthony and the Magic Ring, by Tomie de Paola (Harcourt Brace, 1987)
> Anthony borrows Strega Nona's magic ring to turn himself into a handsome man. He ends up getting more trouble than he bargained for.

Bunnicula, by Deborah Howe and James Howe (Aladdin, 1996)
> Bunnicula seems to be a bit strange, but could he actually be a vampire bunny? (Chapter Book)

Caleb & Kate, by William Steig (Farrar, Straus & Giroux, 1986)
> When Caleb and Kate have a quarrel, Caleb storms out of the house. While he is in the forest resting, a witch turns Caleb into a dog. What will Kate do now?

The Chocolate Touch, by Patrick Skene Catling (Dell, 1996)
> A boy acquires a magical gift that changes everything his lips touch to chocolate. (Chapter Book)

Doctor Change, by Joanna Cole (William Morrow, 1986)
> Evil Dr. Change imprisons his apprentice, Tom, in his home. But Tom learns Dr. Change's spells and makes his escape.

Dog for a Day, by Dick Gackenbach (Clarion Books, 1989)
> A new invention of Sidney's causes unexpected problems when it changes Sidney into his dog and his dog into Sidney.

Dorrie and the Haunted Schoolhouse, by Patricia Coombs (Clarion Books, 1992)
> Dorrie and a fellow student mix up some of their spells and cause chaos in school.

The Frog Prince Continued, by Jon Scieszka (Viking, 1991)
> The Frog Prince and his princess do not live happily ever after, and the Frog decides to find a witch to help him out.

The Garden of Abdul Gasazi, by Chris Van Allsburg (Houghton Mifflin, 1979)
> When Alan lets Miss Hester's dog wander into a magician's garden, he is terrified that the dog has been turned into a duck.

The Growing-up Feet, by Beverly Cleary (Mulberry Books, 1997)
> The twins are disappointed when their feet haven't grown enough to warrant new shoes, but Mr. Markle comes up with another idea.

Humbug Potion, by Lorna Balian (Humbug Books, 1994)
> By learning the letters of the alphabet, you can help a witch decipher the code for a secret recipe that will change her into a beauty.

Imogene's Antlers, by David Small (Crown, 1985)
> When Imogene wakes up one day with antlers growing out of her head, she creates a sensation wherever she goes.

Island Boy, by Barbara Cooney (Puffin Books, 1991)
> Follows the life of Matthias, who grows from a little boy to an old man on a small island.

The Magic Porridge Pot, by Paul Galdone (Houghton Mifflin, 1979)
> An old woman gives a little girl a magic pot that produces all the porridge she and her mother need to survive. The pot runs amuck when the mother tries to use it without knowing the magic words.

Martin's Hats, by Joan W. Blos (Mulberry Books, 1984)
> Martin has many different adventures around his house simply by changing hats.

Meanwhile, Back at the Ranch, by Trinka Hakes Noble (Puffin Books, 1992)
> A rancher who is bored with his everyday life drives to town to find excitement, not knowing the changes that are happening to his wife and ranch while he is away.

The Mixed-up Chameleon, by Eric Carle (HarperCollins Juvenile Books, 1998)
> A little chameleon is unhappy with his looks and wishes that he had different parts of many different animals.

A Murder for Her Majesty, by Beth Hilgartner (Houghton Mifflin, 1992)
> After seeing her father murdered, 11-year-old Alice hides from Queen Elizabeth I by disguising herself as a choirboy in the Yorkshire cathedral. (Chapter Book)

My Teacher Glows in the Dark, by Bruce Coville (Minstrel Books, 1991)
> A student is not sure what to do when he discovers that his new teacher glows. (Chapter Book)

The Paper Crane, by Molly Bang (Greenwillow Books, 1985)
> A stranger pays for his meal in a restaurant with a paper crane that suddenly comes alive.

Puss in Boots, by Paul Galdone (Houghton Mifflin, 1983)
> When his cat outwits a giant by making him change into different animals, a poor man gains fortune and meets a beautiful princess.

Sarah's Unicorn, by Bruce Coville (J. B. Lippincott, 1987)
> Aunt Mag's spell bombs and turns her into a wicked witch who treats her niece, Sarah, badly.

The Shrinking of Treehorn, by Florence Parry Heide (Holiday House, 1992)
> A young boy finds that he is shrinking, but has trouble convincing his parents that it is true. He finds that he must handle the problem by himself.

Sidney Rella and the Glass Sneaker, by Bernice Myers (Houghton Mifflin, 1995)
> Sidney Rella asks his fairy godfather to help him become a football player.

Solomon, the Rusty Nail, by William Steig (Farrar, Straus & Giroux, 1987)
> A bunny with a special ability finds himself in an ominous predicament.

Strega Nona's Magic Lessons, by Tomie de Paola (Harcourt Brace, 1988)
> Anthony disguises himself as a woman so he can learn magic from Strega Nona.

Sylvester and the Magic Pebble, by William Steig (Simon & Schuster, 1989)
> A donkey with a magic pebble asks it to turn him into a rock, then he cannot hold the pebble to turn back to normal.

Touch the Moon, by Marion Dane Bauer (Clarion Books, 1987)
> Jennifer's disappointment at receiving only a china horse for her birthday disappears when the china horse transforms into a magical palomino that can talk and knows a great deal about Jennifer and her father. (Chapter Book)

Two Shoes, New Shoes, by Shirley Hughes (Lothrop, Lee & Shepard, 1986)
> In rhyming text, describes the fun two children have dressing up in unusual shoes, clothes, and hats.

Walk in Wolf Woods, by Mary Stewart (Fawcett, 1989)
> A brother and sister follow a crying man in a strange costume into the woods. They soon find themselves trying to help a fourteenth-century werewolf. (Chapter Book)

Weird Wolf, by Margery Cuyler (Henry Holt, 1991)
> Harry's friend, Abby, helps him break the curse that turned him into a werewolf. (Chapter Book)

Wretched Stone, by Chris Van Allsburg (Houghton Mifflin, 1991)
> A strange stone that glows has a transforming effect on the crew that finds it.

You Be Me, I'll Be You, by Pili Mandelbaum (Kane/Miller Books, 1993)
> A white father and his brown-skinned daughter experiment to see if they would like having each other's skin color.

You're a Little Kid with a Big Heart, by Bernard Waber (Houghton Mifflin, 1980)
> A seven-year-old girl gets her wish to be an adult, only to find that being grown-up is not what she thought it would be.

The following books are out of print, but may be available at the local library.

The Fairy with the Long Nose, by Claude Boujon (Margaret K. McElderry, 1987)
> A fairy gets more than she bargained for when she tries to use her magic to make her long nose smaller.

I Wish I Were There, by Genevieve Laurencin (G. P. Putnam's Sons, 1987)
> A young boy wishes that he could change into different animals to fit different occasions.

It's Just Me, Emily, by Anna Grossnickle Hines (Clarion Books, 19987)
> A little girl pretends to be different animals while her mother tries to guess what they are.

Joe on Sunday, by Tony Blundell (Dial Books for Young Readers, 1987)
> Depending on how he feels, Joe may act like a lion, a pig, a mouse, or some other animal.

King Change-a-Lot, by Babette Cole (G. P. Putnam's Sons, 1989)
> With help from a genie, Prince Change-a-Lot makes many changes to the kingdom which improve the lot of the people.

The Little Lump of Clay, by Diana Engel (Morrow Junior Books, 1989)
> A little lump of clay has its wish granted when a little girl molds him into "something."

A Million Chameleons, by James Young (Little, Brown, 1990)
> A million chameleons enjoy a trip to the zoo, changing color as they move from one activity to another.

Rocking-Horse Land, by Laurence Housman (Lothrop, Lee & Shepard, 1990)
> The rocking horse that Prince Freedling receives for his fifth birthday becomes real during the night and wishes to be set free.

Wretched Stone, by Chris Van Allsburg (Houghton Mifflin, 1991)
> A strange stone that glows has a transforming effect on the crew that finds it.

■ Science Activities

Cement

Tell your students that cement undergoes a chemical change when water is added. When we add water, new chemicals are made which bind together and harden. This process is called "curing." Demonstrate curing in class using the following experiment. You will need plaster of Paris (from a hardware store), water, and an old bowl. (If students do this at home, they will need the help of a parent.)

- Read the directions on the plaster of Paris and mix up 1 cup. Stir the mixture for about five minutes until it is very thick. Press the plaster of Paris into the bottom of the bowl and gently pour (a small trickle at a time) 2–3 cups of water over the plaster of Paris. Let this mixture set for about an hour.
- After an hour, pour off the water and show the class what is inside. Explain that new chemicals were formed with the plaster of Paris when you added water. By overmixing the plaster of Paris and water, you created heat that sped up the hardening process.

Evaporation

To demonstrate whether all liquids evaporate at the same rate, rub some alcohol on the back of a student's left hand and rub some water on the back of that student's right hand. Ask the student: Do the liquids evaporate at the same time? Did one hand feel cooler than the other? Explain that the faster a liquid evaporates, the faster it cools things, because the liquid is taking heat from your body. Ask the class if they can guess how this information can be helpful to medical personnel. (An alcohol rub can cool someone on a hot day or bring down the body temperature of someone with a fever.)

Yeast

Take the class to visit a bakery to observe bread being made or make your own in class. You could also make pizza! (Both bread and pizza dough use yeast.) Have the students write a story about the experience describing the changes the dough went through during the preparation and baking of the bread and explaining why it happened.

Condensation

You can show the students the physical change from a gas to a liquid by demonstrating condensation as follows:

- In a saucepan, heat water until it is boiling. Over the saucepan, hold a pane of glass, a mirror, or a cookie sheet. Point out the water vapor condensing on the surface of the object. You can also heat water in a test tube by holding it over a candle. Ask the students to explain where the water on the sides of the test tube comes from.
- Ask the students if they can explain why the water vapor condenses on the object. (The object cools the water vapor to a temperature less than 212 degrees Fahrenheit/100 degrees Celsius.)

Popping Corn

- Have a popcorn-making demonstration. Record your students' observations of an unpopped kernel of popcorn: What do the kernels weigh? How do they look, feel, and smell? Could they be easily eaten? (Don't let them actually try to eat one!)
- Pop the kernels (use a glass pan, if possible). Ask the students: How do the kernels appear now? What do they weigh? Can you easily eat them? (Definitely let them try to eat these!)
- Ask the students: Was the popcorn undergoing a chemical or physical change during popping (physical)? What caused the change? (As heat was added, the water inside the kernels became steam, and the pressure built up until the kernels "exploded.")

Using Graphing and Prediction Skills

- Combine graphing practice and prediction skills with this exercise. Measure out 1/4 cup of water and place it in a flask or saucepan. Heat the water, keeping track of how long it takes for the water to boil. Ask the students to predict how long it will take for 1/2 cup of water to come to a boil. (Repeat this exercise with 1 cup, 2 cups, 4 cups, etc.)
- After you have determined the results of each exercise, graph the students' predictions and the actual results for each measurement of water. Discuss how accurate the students' predictions were.

Sugar

Place a teaspoon of sugar in a metal spoon and hold it over a flame. Point out to the students the changes that occur. After allowing the remains to cool, have a student taste the substance and ask him or her: Does it taste like sugar? Did the heat cause a physical or a chemical change? (A chemical change occurs as the heat causes the sugar molecules to lose the oxygen and hydrogen atoms, leaving mostly carbon.)

Solids

To demonstrate whether all solids melt at the same temperature, in a frying pan, place several solids (ice, butter, sugar, wax, shortening). Heat the pan slowly. Ask the students: Which solid melts first? How can the fact that solids melt at different temperatures be useful? (The melting point of a substance can be used for identification, the process of melting a substance is often used by industries to separate and purify material, and industries use the knowledge of which substances can withstand intense heat when making decisions about which materials to use in the construction of machinery parts, etc.)

The States of Matter

- Discuss the three states of matter and ask students to come up with several examples of each. Ask them what one way is there to tell if an object is a solid, liquid, or gas. (Solids maintain a constant shape and volume in different containers. Liquids assume the exact shape of their containers and maintain a constant volume. Gases change their shape and volume in different containers.)
- Ask students how you can change a liquid to a gas. Choose a liquid other than water and ask students to predict at what temperature it will solidify and at what temperature it will evaporate. To test your liquid to find out the actual temperatures, do one or both of the following demonstrations:
  1. Place a thermometer in the liquid and place it in a freezer. Check the liquid periodically and record the temperature at which it freezes.
  2. Place some liquid in a pan or flask and heat it until the liquid boils. Record the temperature again. (Be sure the thermometer is not resting on the bottom of the container.)
- Have the students list several examples of liquids. Gather several liquid samples such as water, milk, cola, fruit juice, and flavored drink mix (reconstituted). Place the same amount of each type of liquid in separate, identical containers (plastic glasses or test tubes). Place the samples in the freezer.
- Have the students check the samples every 10–15 minutes and record their observations. Ask them: Did all of the liquids freeze at the same time? Which liquid froze first (water)? What was the freezing point for each liquid? (When did the liquid turn into a solid?) Why did the other liquids take longer to freeze than the water? (The added ingredients in the other liquids lowered the freezing point.) Do these liquids boil at the same temperature?

The Water's Rising!

In a small, glass jar, stuff some steel wool. Put in enough so that you can invert the jar and the steel wool stays in place. Fill a saucer with water and place the inverted jar on the saucer. Have the class observe it daily for one week. Ask them to explain why the water rises. (As the rust forms, it uses oxygen. As the oxygen is used, the pressure inside the jar decreases. The outside pressure is greater than the pressure inside the jar, so the water is forced into the jar.)

Alchemists

Explain to the students that for many centuries, alchemists tried to turn iron into gold. Have the class research this phenomenon to determine the thinking behind this belief and to read about some famous alchemists. Have students pick one of the alchemists they read about and write a biographical paragraph about him or her. (*Strega Nona's Magic Lessons* by de Paola)

Solutions

- As a demonstration, add a spoonful of sugar to a glass of water and stir vigorously. Point out that nothing settles to the bottom. Repeat this process with powdered milk, instant coffee, and powdered drink mix, pointing out the results each time. Explain to the students that when a solid dissolves in a liquid and stays dissolved, the result is a solution.
- Reverse the process by taking a solution (such as salt and water) and pouring it into a pie pan. Heat the solution on a hot plate or in an oven. When all of the water evaporates, ask the students what is left. (The dissolved substance—salt, but not necessarily in its original form.)

Physical or Chemical?

This is a quick activity that you can do to demonstrate the difference between physical and chemical changes.

- Take a piece of paper and wad it into a ball. Ask the students what you have (paper). Cut it into pieces. Ask them what you have now (still paper).
- Burn the paper. (Be sure to have a pan of water close by or burn it in a metal pan.) Ask the students what you have now (ashes). Explain to students that a new substance is formed, and a chemical change has taken place.

Physical Changes

Have students look at a few grains of salt under a magnifying glass and then taste the salt. Then perform the following steps:

- Put a teaspoon of salt into a serving spoon and grind it up with the other spoon. Ask the students: How does it look now? How does it taste? Is this a physical or chemical change?
- Put this powder into a test tube or jar of water and shake it until the salt disappears. (You may need to add more water.) Have a student taste the water. Ask the class: Has the chemical composition of the salt changed?
- Put the salt solution in a saucepan and boil it until the water is gone. Ask the students what is left in the pan and have them taste it.
- Explain to the class that none of the changes altered the chemical composition of the salt. The changes were all physical ones.

It's a Mystery!

Use chemistry to solve a mystery. Label four cups or beakers with the numbers 1, 2, 3, and 4. Tell the students that you have put powdered sugar in cup 1, cornstarch in cup 2, and baking soda in cup 3, but you can't remember what is in cup 4. You do know it is one of the three powders that you put in the first three cups. (You can give students the same mystery powder, or they can have different ones.) For each of the powders, you will perform four tests. Students should make a chart to carefully record their data and determine the mystery powder.

- Test One (Vinegar)—On one section of an egg carton (or paper plate), place a small amount of powder #1 (about 1/4 teaspoon). Add three or four drops of vinegar. Repeat with powders 2, 3, and 4, using a different section of the egg carton each time.
- Test Two (Iodine)—In another section of the carton, place about 1/2 teaspoon of powder #1. Add two or three drops of iodine. Repeat with powders 2, 3, and 4.
- Test Three (Red Cabbage Juice)—Again, on a different section of the egg carton, place about 1/2 teaspoon of powder #1. Add 2 teaspoons of red cabbage juice. (Red cabbage juice is made by boiling one head of red cabbage—cut up—in four quarts of water. Use the juice within two or three days of making it. Store it in the refrigerator. This juice can be used to test if other substances are acid or basic, too.) Repeat with powders 2, 3, and 4.
- Test Four (Flame)—In a metal spoon, place 1/2 teaspoon of powder #1. Hold the spoon with a potholder over a candle. Observe. Repeat with powders 2, 3, and 4.

Ask the students: What is your mystery powder? Have them write up their conclusions in paragraph form using their data to support their findings.

The Onion Story

- Ask the students if they have ever noticed that slicing up an onion can make them cry. Explain that this is caused by a chemical change taking place. Onions contain several chemicals, one of which is called allinase. As you cut the onion, the allinase mixes with air and makes propanethial oxide. Propanethial oxide turns into a vapor, or fumes, and that is what travels into our eyes and nose and causes the burning and tears.
- Tell students to try these two methods when cutting an onion (with adult supervision):
    1. Place an onion in the refrigerator for at least two hours. Take it out of the refrigerator and cut it up immediately. (Cold things do not evaporate as quickly as those that are room temperature. The onion should produce fewer vapors.)
    2. Place enough water in a bowl or pan to cover the onion. Cut up the onion while holding it under the water. (The vapors that form will be dissolved in the water and never reach your eyes.)

Oxidation

Explain to students that many fruits undergo a browning process when exposed to air. This is caused when the oxygen in the air reacts with the enzymes in the fruit. Demonstrate this process as follows:

- Cut an apple into six slices and slice a banana into 1/2-inch pieces (12 pieces). Take one apple wedge and two banana slices and dip them into the following liquids for five seconds: lemon juice, pineapple juice, a commercial fruit preservative (ascorbic acid), a solution of 1/2 teaspoon salt in 1/4 cup water, a solution of 3 tablespoons sugar in 1/4 cup water and no treatment. Label each fruit group after it has been treated and let it sit for one hour. While you are waiting, have the children predict which solutions they think will retard the browning process.

- After one hour, check each fruit group and record the results. Ask the students which liquids slowed the browning process. Discuss what is present in a particular liquid that helped prevent browning. (Lemon juice and commercial preservatives are acidic and act as antioxidants. Pineapple juice contains sulfhydryl groups that retard oxidation.) Explain to the students that the same process is taking place in meat when it begins to look brown after being set out in the air.

- *Challenge Question:* Why don't canned fruits brown? (Heat treatment kills the enzymes.) Compare several canned fruits with fresh fruits. How do they differ?

■ Creative Writing Activities

Following are instructions to give the students for various writing activities.

- Imagine that you wake up one morning to find that you have shrunk to only 6 inches in height. How do you think you would feel being so small? How would you get through a "normal" day at this height? Write a journal of your experiences and explain how you finally remedy the situation. (*The Shrinking of Treehorn* by Heide)

- Many animals undergo physical changes as they grow: the emergence of antlers, a change in coloring, metamorphosis, and so forth. Choose an animal you find interesting and write a magazine article featuring your animal and the physical changes it undergoes during its lifetime.

- People often say they have changed or would like to change. Often the person is not talking about a chemical or physical change, but a character change, such as becoming more patient, controlling his or her temper, or breaking a bad habit. If you could change any characteristic about yourself, what would it be? Write a letter to yourself describing the change you would like and giving the reasons why you think the change is needed. Is there a physical characteristic about yourself that you would like to change? If so, what is it, and why? (*The Fairy with the Long Nose* by Boujon)

- Imagine that you had the ability to make one of your toys come to life. Which toy would you choose? Why would you want that particular toy to come to life? Write a story telling what happens as a result of this transformation. (*Rocking-Horse Land* by Housman; *Babushka's Doll* by Polacco; *Touch the Moon* by Bauer)

- Have you ever wished that you were someone other than who you are? If you could be anyone, whom would you choose to be? Write a magazine article explaining who you would like to be, and why.

- One day, while rummaging around in your grandmother's attic, you find a strange cookbook. All the foods and beverages listed in the cookbook claim to bring about some kind of transformation in the person who eats or drinks them. Although you believe that the book is just for fun, you decide to prepare and sample some of the recipes it contains. Write an account of your experiences while experimenting with this potent cookbook. As an addition to this exercise, prepare your own magical recipe, giving the title of the recipe, the ingredients it contains, and the results of eating or drinking the final product. You can put together a magical cookbook with your classmates.

- You have been working on a special invention that allows two beings to switch places with each other (occupy each other's bodies) for a period of time. The invention is close to completion. One day, while you are having lunch, an unauthorized person starts to fiddle with your machine. Complete this scenario, telling who happened upon your invention and what the outcome of the encounter was. (*Dog for a Day* by Gackenbach)

- While walking through the hills close to your home, you and a friend notice a strange vapor rising out of a crack in the ground nearby. You and your friend move in for a closer look. Where is the vapor coming from? What is its purpose? Write an informative article for your neighborhood newspaper telling what you found.

- Strange things are said to happen when the moon is full: People turn into werewolves and vampires, citings of UFOs are made, and so forth. Write your own story about strange changes that occur as the result of a full moon.

- You and a friend are walking home at dusk. You are hurrying along, when you notice something glowing in the patch of trees at the edge of the park. You are compelled to investigate, even though stopping will make you late for dinner. Write a story that revolves around these (or similar) facts. (*My Teacher Glows in the Dark* by Coville)

- Suppose, like King Midas, everything that you touched would turn to gold. Would you be happy or, like King Midas, would you tire of this magic gift? Write a magazine article describing your ability, how you got it, and how you feel about it. (*The Adventures of King Midas* by Banks)

■ Art Activities

Following are instructions to give the students for various art activities.

- Mix up some plaster of Paris according to the directions. Before the plaster hardens, soak a length of string in it (you decide how much string you want to use). Blow up a balloon (or several balloons of different sizes and shapes). Wrap the string soaked in plaster around the balloon until the balloon is almost totally covered (you can try to make a specific design with your string, also). After the plaster hardens, pop the balloon. You have made a lacy decoration that you can hang in your house or use as a holiday decoration. You can paint your ball, too.

- Read *The Mixed-up Chameleon* by Carle. Draw lines to divide a piece of white paper into six boxes. In the first box, draw a picture of any animal. In the next box, draw the same animal but replace one of its features with that of a different animal. Continue this process in each subsequent box, replacing one more feature each time. The last box will contain your own "mixed-up" creature. Cut rectangles out of construction paper that is slightly larger than the boxes you have drawn on. Cut out the white boxes and glue them on to the construction paper rectangles so that some of the construction paper sticks out on all sides (creating a colored border for your drawing). Put the pages together sequentially and staple them together on the left-hand side to make your own "mixed-up" book. You can make an extra rectangle out of construction paper and staple it at the front of the book for a cover.

- Draw a series of pictures that depict a person changing from one form into another (e.g., a child transforming into an adult, a person turning into a werewolf or a vampire, a human being transforming into an alien form).Use a white piece of paper to show the transformation in a series of drawings placed inside separate boxes (similar to a comic strip).

- People can go through many mood changes during the course of a day:—happy, sad, afraid, excited, angry, annoyed. Draw lines to divide a piece of paper into six boxes of equal size. At the bottom of each box, write the name of an emotion. Above the name, paste pictures of animals that represent this emotion in your mind that you have cut out of a magazine. For example, a scampering squirrel could represent feeling excited, or an owl could represent feeling annoyed. (*Joe on Sunday* by Blundell)

- Turn white bond or typing paper into beautiful stationery to use to write to your friends and family. You will need white bond or typing paper, old newspaper, a disposable baking pan, white envelopes, clean rags, two or three colors of enamel oil paints, and a pencil.

1. Cover your work surface with old newspapers to protect it. Then fill the baking pan with water (fill it about three-quarters full).

2. Place several drops of the different colors of paint that you have chosen in the water. Using the pointed end of a pencil, swirl the water (and paint) around until you have the design you want.

3. Lay a sheet of white paper on top of the water and paint. Let it lie on the water for a few seconds, then grasp one corner of the paper and pull it out of the water. Lay the wet paper, paint side up, on a clean rag and let it dry overnight.

4. Do your writing on the white side of the paper. You can repeat the steps above to make matching envelopes, too.

- Read *Bartholomew and the Oobleck* by Dr. Seuss. Using the recipe listed below, make your own Oobleck:

> 1 16-oz. box cornstarch
> 1 1/2 to 1 2/3 cups water
> 5 drops green food coloring
>
> Mix the ingredients with your fingers (lifting the Oobleck from the bottom to the top) until all ingredients are thoroughly mixed. Store your Oobleck covered. If the Oobleck is too thin, allow it to sit, uncovered, so that some of the extra water will evaporate. After working with the mixture for a while, you may need to add some water because it does tend to dry out. Oobleck can be used again and again if stored, covered, in a refrigerator. With your classmates, brainstorm and see how many uses you can come up with for your Oobleck.

- Use a piece of modeling clay to create whatever you want. With your class, discuss how the exact same lump of clay could be changed into many different objects by just adding some imagination. (*The Little Lump of Clay* by Engel)

- Design your own magical hat by getting an old hat and decorating it. You can use fabric or paints, or glue on objects such as sequins, ribbons, and feathers. Orally describe what happens when you wear your hat and demonstrate its abilities to the class. (*Martin's Hats* by Blos)

- Change one picture into another. Select a large, colorful picture from a magazine and tear it into small pieces. Rearrange the pieces to create a new picture. For example, a red dress could become a flower. Try using a challenging picture such as a group of people or an ad for something such as a refrigerator.

- Create a monster out of a Styrofoam cup. Paint a face on the cup with a thick coat of tempera paint to which a little liquid detergent has been added (to help the paint adhere to the cup). After the head is painted, place the cup, right side up, on a piece of foil and put it under a broiler for a few seconds. (Have an adult help you with this step.) Watch your cup change into a monster!

- Make window sunlight catchers. On a piece of waxed paper, place crayon shavings of your favorite colors. This works well if you use many shades of the same color (pink, red, burgundy, etc.). Place another sheet of waxed paper on top and have an adult iron the paper. Watch as the crayon shavings change and the colors blend. Cut a shape out of the waxed paper, such as an apple, flower, or butterfly. Glue yarn along the edges to frame your work and hang it in the window.

• What if you could change your physical appearance and become an animal? Make noises and motions to imitate different animals. See if your teacher and other students can identify the animal you are imitating (*Joe on Sunday* by Blundell; *It's Just Me, Emily* by Hines). You can also dress up in old or unusual clothing and pretend that you are someone totally different than yourself. How do you feel when you are dressed so differently? (Older students should also write a story describing what animal they would like to be, if they could pick any animal, or what person in history they would most like to be. They should be sure to include the reasons for their choices.)

■ Experiment Books

Adventures with Atoms and Molecules, Chemistry Experiments for Young People (Books, I, II, III, IV), by Robert C. Mebane and Thomas R. Rybolt (Enslow, 1995)
> Chemistry experiments for use in the home or school show the properties and behavior of various kinds of atoms and molecules. Each book contains 30 experiments.

Chemistry Experiments for Children, by Virginia L. Mullin (Dover, 1968)
> Focuses on chemicals in the air, chemistry of water, solutions, diffusion and osmosis, crystals, fire, acids, bases, and salts.

Chemistry for Every Kid: 101 Easy Experiments That Really Work, by Janice Van Cleave (John Wiley & Sons, 1992)
> 101 easy experiments introduce chemistry concepts such as matter, force, gas, solutions, heat, and acids/bases.

Cooking Wizardry for Kids, by Margaret Kenda and Phyllis Williams (Barron's Educational Series, 1990)
> Fun food experiments using common kitchen ingredients give new meaning to solutions, gases, acids, and bases.

Cup and Saucer Chemistry, by Nathan Shalit (Dover, 1989)
> Simple experiments, with materials available in the home, reveal basic chemistry principles.

Dr. Zed's Dazzling Book of Science Activities, by Gordon Penrose and Linda Bucholtz-Ross (Owl Communications, 1993)
> An assortment of science activities that require minimum adult supervision.

Experiment with Air, by Bryan Murphy (Lerner, 1992)
> Brief explanations, accompanied by color photographs, describe experiments to learn about air's properties.

Experiment with Water, by Bryan Murphy (Lerner, 1992)
> Brief explanations, with experiments that use household materials to explore water's properties. Accompanied by color photos.

Kitchen Chemistry, by Robert Gardner (Messner, 1989)
> Science experiments involving chemistry that can be done using materials commonly found in the kitchen.

Magic Mud and Other Great Experiments, by Gordon Penrose (Owl Communications, 1996)
> The host of OWL/TV, Dr. Zed, describes easy science experiments, including oobleck, which he calls "Magic Mud."

Mr. Wizard's 400 Experiments in Science, by Don Herbert and Hy Ruchlis (Book Labs, 1983)
> Experiments to learn the principles of liquids and gases, forms of energy, magnetic and electrical energy, motion, and living things.

175 Science Experiments to Amuse and Amaze Your Friends, by Brenda Walpole (Random House, 1991)

>Instructions for 175 experiments, tricks, and creations that illustrate the principles of water, air, movement, and light.

Science Experiments You Can Eat, by Vicki Cobb (HarperCollins, 1994)

>Easy-to-do experiments centering around food preservation, additives, and flavoring.

Science for Kids: 39 Easy Chemistry Experiments, by Robert W. Wood (TAB Books, 1991)

>Thirty-nine simple chemistry experiments show how chemicals can be controlled to produce new materials or forms of energy.

Science Magic for Kids, by William R. Wellnitz, Ph.D. (TAB Books, 1990)

>Over 60 science experiments test the properties of colors, food, air soap bubbles, heat, light, plants, and magnets.

Temperature (Measure up with Science), by Brenda Walpole (Gareth Stevens, 1995)

>Introduces methods of measuring temperature and discusses different factors relating to temperature.

200 Gooey, Slippery, Slimy, Weird, and Fun Experiments, by Janice Van Cleave (John Wiley & Sons, 1992)

>Provides easy-to-understand directions and helpful illustrations for experiments in biology, chemistry, and physics.

200 Illustrated Science Experiments for Children, by Robert J. Brown (TAB Books, 1988)

>Two hundred illustrated science experiments covering air, sound, vibrations, water, surface tension, mechanics, chemistry, light, heat, biology, electricity, and magnetism.

SPACE

- Key Concepts
- Comprehensive Teaching Resources
- Chapter 1: The Universe
- Chapter 2: The Planets
- Chapter 3: The Moon
- Chapter 4: Space Exploration
- Additional Resources

Key Concepts

■ Primary Concepts

Students will be able to:

1. Explain that the sun is a star and provides heat and light (Chapter 1).

2. Differentiate between rotation and revolution of the Earth (Chapter 2).

3. Describe how the rotation of the Earth around the sun causes night and day (Chapter 2).

4. Explain that the Earth and eight other planets orbit the sun (Chapter 2).

5. Describe the different phases of the moon (Chapter 3).

■ Intermediate Concepts

Students will be able to:

1. Contrast the sun with other stars in terms of their physical characteristics (Chapter 1).

2. Name the planets of our solar system and indicate their order in relationship to the sun; construct a scale model of the solar system (Chapter 2).

3. Cite proofs that the Earth rotates on its axis and revolves around the sun (Chapter 2).

4. Compare size and surface features of the moon and Earth (Chapters 2, 3).

5. Identify phases of the moon and explain the reason for each (Chapter 3).

■ Upper Concepts

Students will be able to:

1. Research and record the sun's age, size, distance from the Earth, temperatures, rotation period, composition, gravity, and color, and diagram and label prominent features and layers (Chapter 1).

2. Define a light-year and explain why such a unit is necessary to measure distances in the universe (Chapter 1).

3. Differentiate between solar and lunar eclipses and diagram them (Chapters 2, 3).

4. Describe and identify various constellations and give the location of each; recount the legend associated with each constellation; recognize the brightest and largest stars (Chapter 1).

5. Assess the size, shape, and composition of the Milky Way (Chapter 1).

6. Identify and contrast theories of the origin of our universe and solar system (Chapter 1). (Resource books detailing the religious explanation of creation are listed in the "Additional Resources" section of this unit.)

7. Explain why the Earth is divided into time zones (Chapter 2).

8. Describe the relationship between the rotation of the Earth and the time of day (Chapter 2).

9. Research the following about each planet: distance from the sun; position from the sun (in relation to the other planets); approximate size; lengths of orbit; temperatures; number of moons; possibility of life existing; strength of gravitational pull (Chapter 2).

10. Generalize how planets stay in order in space (Newton's Law) (Chapter 2).

11. Research and record the moon's size, gravity, age, temperature, distance from Earth, revolution period, rotation period, and surface features (Chapter 3).

12. Explain how the Earth and moon act as a system and the natural phenomena that result (Chapters 2, 3).

13. Describe space exploration achievements (e.g., Mercury, Gemini, Apollo, Skylab, the space shuttle, and probes) (Chapter 4).

14. Research and discuss the contributions of famous astronomers; distinguish between Ptolemy's and Copernicus's concepts of the solar system (Chapter 4).

15. Discuss the invention and early development of the telescope; differentiate among refracting, reflecting, and radio telescopes and spectroscopes (Chapter 4).

Comprehensive Teaching Resources

The following table lists books that cover a wide range of topics about space. One of these books could serve as your main teaching guide while studying this unit. Each book is listed with a short summary, and the chapters in this book that it applies to are noted. The books are listed by degree of difficulty, easiest to most difficult.

BOOK AND SUMMARY	AUTHOR	CHAPTERS			
		1	2	3	4
The Nova Space Explorer's Guide (Crown, 1991) Simulates a space trip to the moon and all planets. Also circles Earth and observes it from space.	Richard Maurer		X	X	
Journey to the Planets (Crown, 1993) Explores the planets of our solar system, high-lighting the prominent features of each.	Patricia Lauber		X	X	
The New Book of Popular Science (Grolier, 1998) In textbook style, thoroughly covers the areas of astronomy and space science.	Deluxe Library Edition	X	X	X	X

Each chapter in this section lists reference books that focus on the specific area of space being addressed. These books can be used to complement and expand upon the basic information provided in the comprehensive resource books listed in the previous table.

The reference books in each chapter have been classified by age level to help you select those that best fit the needs and interests of your student(s).

Chapter 1
The Universe

■ Teaching Resources

Books containing experiment(s) relating to the subject matter are marked with a plus sign (+) before and after the title.

P   *Galaxies*, by Paul Sipiera (Children's Press, 1997)
Examines what a galaxy is, the different types that exist, their structures, and some facts learned from the study of galaxies.

P   +*Glow in the Dark Constellations*,+ by C. E. Thompson (Grosset & Dunlap, 1989)
A guide to viewing the constellations for young children.

P   *The Glow-in-the-Dark Night Sky Book*, by Clint Hatchett (Random House, 1988)
Illustrates the night sky during different times of the year.

P   *The Night Sky*, by Robin Kenod (Benchmark Books, 1996)
Describes which stars and constellations can be seen in the night sky and provides instructions for finding them.

P   *Stars*, by Jennifer Dussling (Grosset & Dunlap, 1996)
Explains what stars are and what people have thought about them in different times and places.

P   *The Sun and the Solar System*, by Franklyn M. Branley (Twenty-First Century Books, 1996)
Discusses the solar system, comparing how it was perceived in earlier times with what is known now.

P   *The Sun Is Always Shining Somewhere*, by Allan Fowler (Children's Press, 1992)
Examines the sun in the context of other, more distant stars, and discusses the night sky and the movement of the Earth.

P   +*The Sun, Our Nearest Star*,+ by Franklyn M. Branley (HarperCollins, 2000)
Describes the sun and how it provides the light and energy that allow plant and animal life to exist on the Earth.

P   *Sun Up, Sun Down*, by Gail Gibbons (Harcourt Brace Jovanovich, 1983)
Discusses why we need the sun, the varying effects of the sun as the seasons change, and what would happen to the Earth if there were no sun.

P/I *Comets and Meteors,* by Jeanne Bendick (Millbrook Press, 1994)
Simple answers to children's questions about comets and meteors: What are they? Where do they come from? Where do they go?

P/I *Galaxies,* by Seymour Simon (Mulberry Books, 1991)
Identifies the nature, locations, movements, and different categories of galaxies, examining the Milky Way and other known examples.

P/I *The Long View into Space,* by Seymour Simon (Crown, 1987)
An illustrated discussion of the planets and bodies such as moons, comets, and meteoroids found in our solar system. Also outlines the relationship of the solar system to the galaxies.

P/I *Stars,* by Paul Sipiera (Children's Press, 1997)
Explains the nature, formation, and death of stars.

I *The Sun,* by Seymour Simon (William Morrow, 1986)
Describes the nature of the sun, its origin, source of energy, layers, atmosphere, sun spots, and activity.

I/U +*The Night Sky Book,*+ by Jamie Jobb (Little, Brown, 1977)
An astronomy observer's manual. Contains information, activities, and "tests" to help the reader become familiar with the night sky.

■ Reading Selections

Books marked with an asterisk (*) before and after the title are related to activities in the activity sections of this chapter.

Arrow to the Sun, by Gerald McDermott (Viking, 1974)
> An adaptation of a Pueblo Indian myth, which explains how the spirit of the Lord of the Sun was brought to the world of men. (Sound recording available from Weston Woods, 1991.)

Draw Me a Star, by Eric Carle (Putnam, 1992)
> This is a dreamy story of an artist, who, while drawing a star, a sun, a tree, a house, flowers, and people, discovers not only his art but his life. In the end, it is the star who shows him the universe.

Follow the Drinking Gourd, by Jeanette Winter (Alfred A. Knopf, 1992)
> By following directions in a song taught them by a sailor and watching the night sky, runaway slaves journey along the Underground Railway. (Videocassette available from Great Plains National Instructional Television Library, 1993.)

The Heavenly Zoo: Legends and Tales of the Stars, by Alison Lurie (Farrar, Straus & Giroux, 1996)
> Sixteen legends of the constellations and how they got their names, taken from varied sources such as Ancient Greece, the Bible, Norway, and the American Indians.

Her Seven Brothers, by Paul Goble (Aladdin, 1993)
> Retells a Cheyenne legend in which a girl and her seven chosen brothers become the Big Dipper.

How Many Stars in the Sky, by Lenny Hort (Econo-Clad Books, 1999)
> One night when Mama is away, Daddy and child seek a good place to count the stars in the night sky.

I Have a Friend, by Keiko Narahashi (Aladdin, 1998)
> A small boy tells about his friend who lives with him, follows him, and is sometimes very tall, but disappears when the sun goes down: his shadow.

Lone Star, by Barbara Barrie (Delacorte, 1990)
> Moving from Chicago to Corpus Christi, Texas, in 1944, a young Jewish girl copes with her parents' problems and adopts a new lifestyle that alienates her Orthodox grandfather. (Chapter Book)

Meteor!, by Patricia Polacco (Philomel, 1999)
> A quiet, rural community is dramatically changed when a meteor crashes down in the front yard of the Gaw family.

My House Has Stars, by Megan McDonald (Orchard, 1996)
> Young people around the world describe the kinds of homes they live in and how they see the stars.

The Night Flight, by Joanne Ryder (Aladdin, 1998)
> At night after falling asleep, Anna flies to her favorite park, which is now filled with crocodiles, monkeys, and a lion that takes her to a secret waterfall.

No Star Nights, by Anna Egan Smucker (Alfred A. Knopf, 1994)
> A young girl growing up in a steel-mill town in the 1950s describes her childhood and the effects on it of the local industry.

Shine, Sun!, by Carol Greene (Children's Press, 1983)
> As a child talks to the sun, the reader can see some of the sun's happy effects.

Ship of Dreams, by Dean Morrissey (H. N. Abrams, 1994)
> Joey takes a trip through the star-filled night to help the Sandman place new stars in the sky.

A Song of Stars, by Tom Birdseye (Holiday House, 1990)
> Although banished to opposite sides of the Milky Way, the princess weaver and the herdsman reunite each year on the seventh day of the seventh month.

Spacey Riddles, by Katy Hall (Dial Books for Young Readers, 1992)
> Riddles about the sun, stars, moon, planets, and space travel.

They Dance in the Sky: Native American Star Myths, by Jean Guard Monroe (Houghton Mifflin, 1987)
> A collection of legends about the stars from various North American Indian cultures.

Wake Up, Sun!, by David Lee Harrison (Random House, 1986)
> When Dog wakes up early, in the middle of the night, he launches all the other farm animals on a worried search for the missing sun.

Watch the Stars Come Out, by Riki Levinson (Puffin Books, 1995)
> Grandma tells about her mama's journey to America by boat, years before.

The Way to Start a Day, by Byrd Baylor (Aladdin, 1986)
> Text and illustrations describe how people all over the world celebrate the sunrise.

Where Does the Sun Go at Night?, by Mirra Ginsburg (William Morrow, 1987)
> Every night the sun goes to the house of his grandma, the deep blue sky is tucked in bed by his grandpa, the wind, and is awakened the following day by the morning.

The following books are out of print, but may be available at the local library.

Beyond the Milky Way, by Cecile Schoberle (Crown, 1978)

> Looking out of a city window and seeing the night sky, a child describes the glowing wonder of outer space and imagines another child doing the same thing on a distant planet.

The Boy Who Painted the Sun, by Jill Morris (Penguin, 1983)

> A boy misses his colorful farm when he moves to the city and finds a way to make the city more colorful and make the people smile.

Brother Moukey and the Falling Sun, by Karen Whiteside (Harper & Row, 1980)

> Moukey tries to find a way to deal with his anger at his brother and realizes that the answer is within himself.

Claude and Sun, by Matt Novak (Bradbury Press, 1987)

> From morning till night, Claude and Sun have a wonderful time together.

Louhi, Witch of North Farm, by Toni Gerez (Viking, 1986)

> Louhi's plan to steal the sun and moon backfires when the gods learn of her mischievous scheme.

The Miser Who Wanted the Sun, by Jurg Obrist (Atheneum, 1984)

> Two children teach a greedy miser that he must share certain things.

The Morning the Sun Refused to Rise, by Glen Rounds (Holiday House, 1984)

> When the sun doesn't rise one morning, the King of Sweden contacts Paul Bunyan and asks him to find the cause of the catastrophe.

One Sun: A Book of Terse Verse, by Bruce McMillan (Holiday House, 1990)

> Describes a day at the beach in a series of terse verses (verses made up of two monosyllabic words that rhyme) accompanied by photographs.

Pancho's Pinata, by Stefan Czernecki (Hyperion Books for Children, 1992)

> On Christmas Eve, Pancho rescues a star from a cactus and receives the gift of happiness.

Sky All Around, by Anna Grossnickle Hines (Clarion Books, 1989)

> A father and daughter share a special time when they go out on a clear night to watch the stars.

Star Tales: North American Indian Stories About the Stars, by Gretchen Mayo (Walker, 1990)

> A collection of Indian legends about stars, the moon, and the nighttime sky.

Under the Sun, by Ellen Kandoian (Dodd & Mead, 1987)

> Molly's mother answers her question about where the sun goes each night by taking her on a visual journey around the world.

■ Science Activities

Stars

Tell students that the stars have played an important part in Earth's history: According to the Bible, the stars helped to guide the Wise Men to Jesus, were used for navigation by explorers like Columbus, and helped guide runaway slaves on the Underground Railway. Have them choose one historic event and research it, then write a paper on the event and what part the stars played in it.

Constellations

As a class, make a chart of one of the constellations, placing the stars in their proper positions in the sky. Then have a student draw this constellation's "form" around these stars (e.g., The Big Dipper, The Bear).

Star Symbols

Tell the children that there are many different "star" symbols that we encounter in our daily lives (e.g., the stars on our country's or state's flag, stars we receive from parents or teachers for a job well done, movie stars, the Star of David). Ask the class why they think the symbol or the word *star* is used in each case. Can they think of any other star symbols?

Stars and the Seasons

Have students chart the stars according to the seasons, drawing the winter, spring, summer, and fall skies.

Expand the Universe

- Have the children blow up balloons part way. With a magic marker, they should draw spots all over the balloons, about the same distance apart. Then ask them to blow the balloons up all the way and notice how all the spots have moved away from each other.
- Ask the students to imagine that the skin of their balloons is the universe and the spots are the galaxies. When they blew up the balloons, the spots moved farther apart. Explain that this is what scientists believe is happening in space. The universe is expanding and the galaxies are moving farther apart.

The Night Sky

Ask students if they have seen the night sky both in the country and in the city. Where do they think we can see more stars, and why?

Pollution

Discuss pollution and regulations in force now and in the 1950s. Do students think people are more or less concerned about pollution today? Ask them to describe what is being done to control air pollution today. (*No Star Nights* by Smucker)

Moving Through Space

Have those students who have a telescope at home locate a planet in the night sky by looking through a telescope. They should keep the telescope perfectly still so that they will be able to watch the planet move out of their view. They should then find it again. Explain that this demonstrates the fact that the Earth and the other planets are moving (rotating).

The Sun Losing Its Power

Have students do research on the theory that the sun is losing its power. Do they agree with this theory? Why or why not? Have them find facts to strengthen their opinions.

Eclipse

Have each student hold a ping-pong ball close to his or her eye while looking at a larger object (such as a car, a bus, the school, etc.). They should note that the larger object is totally hidden from view. Use this exercise to explain how the moon, which is much smaller, can block the sun from our view.

Making Scale Models

Have students draw a shape to represent the actual size of the sun, then draw the nine planets to scale and put the Earth's moon in its place, also to scale. They could also make a mobile to scale.

The Earth and the Sun

Ask the students: Which areas of the Earth depend most on the sun? How would the Earth change if all areas received the same amount and intensity of sunlight?

The Sun's Influence on Cultures

- Have the class find out more about the Pueblo Indians, such as in what part of the country they live, what types of arts and crafts they make, and what types of foods they eat (*Arrow to the Sun* by McDermott). Have them research what the Pueblo Indians' beliefs about the sun are and what makes the sun so important to them that adoration of it is part of their religion.
- Have students research and explain how life is different for people living in areas (such as Alaska) where there are months of total daylight and then months of total darkness.

Measuring Distances

Ask the students to find the answers to the following questions:
- What is the distance, in miles, from the Earth to the sun, from the Earth to each of the other eight planets, and from the sun to each of the nine planets?
- What is the speed of light? How long would it take light to reach the Earth (and the other planets) from the sun?

Scaling the Sun

Have the students do the following experiment to understand the size of the sun:
- On a sheet of cardboard, draw a small circle about 3/16-inch across. This will represent the Earth. On a large sheet of cardboard, draw a circle 17 9/16-inches across. (This can be accomplished by tying a pencil to a piece of string. Pin the other end of the string to the middle of the cardboard, 8 3/4" away from the pencil.) This is the sun.
- Stand 100 large steps (about 165 feet) away from another person. One person holds the "Earth" and the other person hold the "sun." This represents the distance and size difference between the sun and the Earth.

■ Creative Writing Activities

Following are instructions to give the students for various writing activities.
- Write a story about a special time you enjoyed with a parent or grandparent. (*Sky All Around* by Hines)

- Write a story about your town and what neighbors might do if a meteor fell in your yard. (*Meteor!* by Polacco)

- On a clear night, go outside and spend a few minutes looking at the night sky. Write down your impressions of how the sky looked and how it made you feel.

- Make up a story in which the moon, sun, or stars have human qualities. What type of person would the moon be? The sun?

- Make up your own legend about how one of the constellations got its name. (*The Heavenly Zoo: Legends and Tales of the Stars* by Lurie; *They Dance in the Sky: Native American Star Myths* by Monroe; *Star Tales: North American Indian Stories About the Stars* by Mayo)

- Write a story about being lost (in the woods, on a mountain, in the snow) and using the North Star (Polaris) to find your way to safety.

- Pretend that you are a celebrity, or a "star." What are you famous for? What is your life like? What would you change about your life if you could? Write a letter to a young fan either encouraging or discouraging him or her from becoming a "star."

- Write a poem about a star on fancy paper. Draw stars along the border and send it to someone special.

- Write a story about a star that falls to Earth and needs help getting back to the heavens. Who does the star ask for help? Who finally helps it? How does it get back home?

- There is something wrong in the universe! The planets are slowly changing course and no one knows exactly why. Scientists fear that one or more of them may collide! Write news stories covering this event. What finally happens?

- Read *Brother Mouky and the Falling Sun* by Whiteside. Write a letter to Mouky suggesting different ways he might deal with his anger at his brother. What do you do when you are angry?

- Cut out pictures and write terse verses to describe something in the pictures. Your verses can be made into a book or a mini-poster. (*One Sun: A Book of Terse Verse* by McMillan)

- Write a story pretending that you are the sun. What do you see on the different areas of the Earth as the world spins? How does it feel knowing so many people, animals, and plants depend on you for life?

- Write a paper about a planned trip to the sun. Could you actually land on the sun? What would happen to your spaceship? What would happen to you? If your spaceship could protect you, what would you find on the sun?

- Write a story describing what activities you would want the sun to join you in and how the warmth of the sun could add to the activity. (*Claude and Sun* by Novak)

- Write about what it would be like if you had to live inside a cave for three months without ever seeing the sun. Research actual experiments in which people have lived like this (in caves or underground). What were the results?

- Write a story about a boy who misses the city when he goes to spend a week on a farm. What areas of the city would he miss most? (*The Boy Who Painted the Sun* by Morris)

- Write a story about what the day would be like if the sun didn't rise. How would you feel? How would it change your daily activities?

- Write a story about your activities on a given day, from getting up in the morning to going to bed at night. Did any of your activities depend on the sun shining?

- Write your own version of *Where Does the Sun Go at Night?* by Ginsburg. Where would you have the sun spend its nights?

- How does a sunset make you feel? Write a story about a child who sets out to stop the sun from setting by tricking it. What happens as a result? How would it affect the calendar?

- Write a story about a person who discovers a way to "bottle" sunshine. What does he or she do with the discovery? Do they share it or keep it to themselves? How do other people feel about the discovery?

- How would you feel living in a part of the Earth that receives six months of continual sunlight or darkness (as in Alaska)? How would this affect your activities? Would your lifestyle change at all? Write a letter to a friend expressing your feelings.

- If you could have any wish you want, what would you wish for yourself? What would you wish for your family? What would you wish for the world? Write and illustrate a poem that expresses what your wish would be. (Following is a copy of the traditional "Wishing Star" poem):

Star Light, Star Bright,
First Star I See Tonight.
I Wish I May,
I Wish I Might,
Have the Wish I Wish Tonight.

■ Art Activities

Following are instructions to give the students for various art activities.

- Make a "night" hanging. Punch holes in black paper with a straight pin to resemble stars. Make the holes in any pattern or design you want. Hang the paper in a window so the light can shine through. You can also tape the paper to the open end of an empty can that has had the bottom and top removed from it. Look through the open end while holding the can up to the window or to a light.

- What songs do you know about stars ("Twinkle, Twinkle Little Star," "Catch a Falling Star")? Write a song about a star. Write new words to a familiar melody or make up your own melody.

- Using black construction paper, cut out small stars and a moon shape to make the pattern of a night sky on the paper. Hold the construction paper up and shine a lamp or flashlight through the holes you've made in the paper. A night "sky" will be projected onto the wall in your house.

- Make a picture of the night sky and glue it to a piece of cardboard. Tape a flap onto the back of the cardboard so it will stand up like a picture frame does. Glue objects on the night sky scene (mountains, people, spaceships, etc.) to create a picture. Repeat this process and create a day-time scene. This can also be done inside a box (like a shoe box) that has had one end cut out and covered with clear or colored plastic wrap to make a diorama.

- Draw a picture of an old-time sailing ship at night navigating by the stars. Include clues in the picture that point to where the ship is headed or where it came from. See if your family can guess the ship's destination or point of origin.

- Draw a picture of you in your pajamas flying through the night sky. What would you be riding on? Where would you go?

- Design what you think a "wishing star" would look like. How would you make it stand out?

- Design your own constellation. Which sky would it be in (summer, fall, winter, spring)? What would you name it?

- Create a star "family." Make the stars all slightly different so that you can tell them apart. What constellation are they part of?

- Make a night picture by coloring a piece of paper yellow. Then color over the yellow with a black crayon, using thick strokes. Using a sharp object (like a nail file) "engrave" a picture by etching off the black and allowing the yellow to show through.

- Draw a picture of a starfish. Can you make other animals from a star shape?

- Draw a picture of a place at sunset and again at noon. How will the pictures differ? Think about shadow sizes and placements.

- Using a paper plate, paint a sun face on one side and a moon face on the other side. You could mount the plate on a stick and use it in a play about the sun and the moon.

- Draw a picture of the sun as a fiery ball, using different colors to make it look hot and fiery. Then draw a picture of the sun as it usually looks in books and pictures. Use crayons, markers, finger-paints, or watercolors. Which picture gives the best sensation of a very hot, fiery sun?

- Draw a picture using only warm colors (red, orange, and yellow). What did you choose to draw? Why?

- Draw silhouettes of your family. Turn on one lamp in a dark room and have a family member sit in front of the lamp. This will create a shadow on the wall. Trace this silhouette on a piece of paper that has been hung on the wall.

- Draw a picture of what you think a "Sun Festival" would look like. Before making your picture, think about what colors you should use, how the people would be dressed, and what activities they would be participating in. (*The Way to Start a Day* by Baylor)

- Often, faces are drawn on the sun in a picture. Draw several different scenes with different faces on the sun. How does the sun's face affect your scene? How does the scene affect your sun's face?

- Color a paper plate to resemble the sun (you can put a face on it, if you want to). With a hole punch (or an adult can use a scissors), make some holes in the edge of the plate. Make two holes, one inch apart, then leave a space about 2 1/2 inches long and make two more holes, 1 inch apart. Continue this pattern around the entire plate. Using red, orange, and/or yellow pipe cleaners, make the sun's "rays." Attach each end of the pipe cleaner to one of the holes spaced 1 inch apart.

Chapter 2
The Planets

■ Teaching Resources

Books containing experiment(s) relating to the subject matter are marked with a plus sign (+) before and after the title.

P   *The Planets,* by Gail Gibbons (Holiday House, 1993)
Discusses the movements, location, and characteristics of the nine known planets in our solar system.

P/I *The Earth,* by Cynthia Pratt Nicolson (Kids Can Press, 1999)
Forty pages of illustrations and information about the Earth.

P/I *The Magic School Bus Lost in the Solar System,* by Joanna Cole (Scholastic, 1993)
On a special field trip, Ms. Frizzle's class goes into outer space and visits each planet in the solar system.

P/I *Mars,* by Michael George (Child's World, 1997)
Describes what has been discovered about the intriguing red planet, from the early days of the Romans until now.

P/I *Planet Earth,* by Martyn Bramwell (Quadillion, 2000)
Explains all about the Earth: relationships with the moon and sun, the seasons, and plant and animal life.

I   *Jupiter,* by Mary Ann McDonald (Child's World, 1998)
Describes the location, movements, surface, and moons of Jupiter.

I   *Jupiter,* by Seymour Simon (William Morrow, 1988)
Describes the characteristics of the planet Jupiter and its moons as revealed by photographs sent back by two unmanned Voyager spaceships.

I   *Mars,* by Seymour Simon (Mulberry Books, 1990)
Book includes text and photographs describing features of the red planet.

I   *Neptune,* by Elaine Landau (Franklin Watts, 1996)
Uses photographs and other recent findings to describe the atmosphere and geographic features of Neptune.

I   *Neptune,* by Seymour Simon (Mulberry Books, 1997)
Discusses the physical features and moons of Neptune and how we have gained our knowledge of this giant world.

I   *Saturn,* by Seymour Simon (William Morrow, 1988)
Describes the sixth planet from the sun, its rings and its moons, and includes photographs taken in outer space.

I   *Uranus,* by Seymour Simon (Mulberry Books, 1990)
Introduces, through text and photographs, the characteristics of Uranus.

I   *Venus,* by Seymour Simon (Morrow Junior Books, 1992)
Describes the movements and physical features of Venus and recent findings about its climate and surface.

I/U *Saturn,* by Elaine Landau (Franklin Watts, 1991)
Using recent findings and photographs, this book presents information about Saturn's atmosphere and geographic features.

I/U *Seeing Earth from Space,* by Patricia Lauber (Orchard, 1990)
Text and photographs taken from space depict the nature, evolution, and future of Earth.

■ Reading Selections

Books marked with an asterisk (*) before and after the title are related to activities in the activity sections of this chapter.

Earth Hounds as Explained by Professor Xargle, by Jeanne Willis (Dutton Children's Books, 1990)
   An alien teaches his class about the dog species.

Earth Tigerlets as Explained by Professor Xargle, by Jeanne Willis (Dutton Children's Books, 1991)
   An alien teaches his class about the cat species.

Merry Christmas, Space Case, by James Marshall (E. P. Dutton, 1989)
   Buddy McGee eagerly awaits a promised Christmas visit from his friend, the thing from outer space.

My Place in Space, by Robin Hirst (Orchard, 1992)
   Henry tells the bus driver exactly where he lives, positioning himself precisely in the universe.

The Pool of Fire, by John Christopher (Aladdin, 1988)
   Will and the small group of free people carry out a clever and perilous plan to destroy the Master's three great cities before a spaceship destined to doom the planet arrives. (Chapter Book)

Space Case, by Edward Marshall (Dial, 1992)
   When the thing from outer space visits Earth, it is mistaken first for a trick-or-treater and then for a robot. (Video recording available from Great Plains National Television, 1986.)

The Talking Earth, by Jean Craighead George (Harper Trophy, 1987)
   Billie Wind ventures out alone into the Florida Everglades to test the legends of her Indian ancestors and learns the importance of listening to the Earth's vital messages. (Chapter Book)

Zebo and the Dirty Planet, by Kim Fernandes (Annick Press, 1991)
   Zebo saves the animals from the polluted Earth by taking them to his planet.

The following books are out of print, but may be available at the local library.

Alistair in Outer Space, by Marilyn Sadler (Prentice-Hall, 1984)
When Alistair is kidnapped by a spaceship full of Goots from Gootula, his main concern is for his overdue library books.

Beyond the Milky Way, by Cecile Schoberle (Crown, 1986)
Looking out of a city window and seeing the night sky, a child describes the glowing wonder of outer space and imagines another child doing the same thing on a distant planet.

Ellsworth and the Cats from Mars, by Patience Brewster (Houghton Mifflin, 1981)
An ordinary young cat is visited by green-haired cats from Mars who want to study the ways of earthly felines.

Planet Was, by Amy Boesky (Little, Brown, 1990)
The royal policy on Planet Was is never to change anything, until the young Prince Pierre decides that change would be fun and takes matters into his own hands.

A Trip to Mars, by Ruth Young (Orchard, 1990)
A small child prepares for a trip to Mars, making sure to pack space gloves, space glasses, and a space teddy bear.

The Turning Place, by Jean E. Karl (E. P. Dutton, 1976)
Nine short stories reveal various aspects of future life on Earth and other planets. (Chapter Book)

Wally, the Worry-Warthog, by Barbara Shook Hazen (Clarion, 1990)
Wally, a warthog who worries about everything, like little green men from Mars, discovers that the terrifying Wilberforce has a many fears as he does.

■ Science Activities

Solar System Mobile

Have students make a mobile of the solar system (including the sun and the nine planets). More advanced students can include some of the moons that orbit the planets.

Planet Mobile

Have students build a mobile showing just one of the nine planets. They should include all moons associated with the chosen planet.

Picture the Planets

Have students make individual pictures showing what they think each of the nine planets looks like on its surface. As a class, discuss what the planets are made up of, what their atmospheres are like, and why they depicted them as they did. On the back of each picture, students should write a short summary of what the planet is actually made up of and information about its atmosphere. These sheets could then be bound into a book with a cover designed by the students.

Planet Areas

Tell the students the diameter of each planet and have them determine the radius of each, the area of a cross-section of the planet (the area of a circle), the circumference of each, and the surface area of the planet (the surface area of a sphere). The planets and their diameters (to the nearest 100 km.) are listed below:

Mercury: 4,900 km

Venus: 12,000 km

Earth: 12,800 km

Mars: 6,800 km

Jupiter: 139,800 km

Saturn: 116,500 km

Uranus: 50,700 km

Neptune: 48,900 km

Pluto: 3,000 km

Planet Discovery

Have students discover their own planets. They should place them in the solar system and give them names. Ask them to describe what their planets are made of and what their atmospheres are like. They should also determine what kind of plant and animal life exists there and describe what life on their planets would be like. (Amend this project to suit the age(s) of the children you are teaching.)

Gravity

Have one student at a time do the following activity outside in a large, open area, under your supervision:

- Put a small rubber ball into the toe of a stocking. Hold on to the open end of the stocking and spin the ball around your head.
- Can you feel the ball trying to pull away? To keep it moving, you have to pull it in the other direction. This is how a planet travels around the sun. The planet tries to escape, but the sun pulls on it to keep it in place. This is a result of the sun's gravity.
- Whirl the ball around again. Let it go. What happens? Does the ball fly off in a circle or a straight line? This is what would happen if the force of gravity stopped.

Magic School Bus Ride

Have students take a "Magic School Bus" ride across the solar system. They can describe their journey into a tape recorder, creating appropriate sound effects to accompany the tale. Ask them to be sure to give detailed descriptions of the planets they visit. They can also interview classmates or relatives for additional stories. (*The Magic School Bus Lost in the Solar System* by Cole)

■ Creative Writing Activities

Following are instructions to give the students for various writing activities.

- Choose a planet and write a story about what it might be like living on that planet.
- Some planets have more than one moon. Would you prefer to have one moon or many moons? Explain why.
- Write a story about a time you were lost or afraid. (*Ellsworth and the Cat from Mars* by Brewster)
- Write your own poem about Planet Was. (*Planet Was* by Boesky)
- Describe what you think the Earth will be like in the year 2100. What will everyday life be like? What will people do for fun?
- What if all the planets' orbits were the same? Would we be in danger of bumping into each other? Write about some of the advantages and disadvantages of this imaginary solar system.

- The Earth's orbit is the perfect distance from the sun for human habitation. What would happen if a natural disaster should "shake" us out of our orbit and move us into an orbit farther away from or closer to the sun? Write a story about how life would change and people and animals would adjust.

- Write a story about visiting another planet in an imaginary solar system. What is the name of the planet you visited? What type of beings lived there? Was your imaginary planet similar to Earth, or very different? What did you like best about your planet? What didn't you like?

- You suspect that the new kid in school is from another planet. You decide to make friends and investigate. Write a journal of your daily encounters with this new friend (include your findings and conclusions).

- You work for a company that offers the first commercial flights to outer space and vacations on other planets. Write a brochure for your company advertising its vacation packages. You can use real or made-up planets.

■ Art Activities

Following are instructions to give the students for various art activities.

- Using clay, create a scene of life on another planet. Include a person, or an animal, and its habitat. (*Zebo and the Dirty Planet* by Fernandes)

- Read *Alistair in Outer Space* by Sadler. Paint a picture of Goots and his planet.

- Design a vehicle that could travel on a planet of your choice (other than Earth). What special features would it need to travel the terrain and atmosphere of your planet? What fuel would it use? How large would it be? You can draw a picture of your vehicle, make it out of discarded material around the house, or mold it out of clay.

- Create a plant from another planet. Name it and tell where you discovered it growing. Describe its special features that were necessary for it to survive on its planet. How will you enable it to survive on Earth? You can draw the plant or make it out of construction or tissue paper, toilet paper rolls, blocks, or tin cans,.

- Read *Earth Tigerlets as Explained by Professor Xargle* or *Earth Hounds as Explained by Professor Xargle* by Willis. Paint a picture of a tigerlet or Earth hound.

- Create a travel poster promoting a visit to another planet during a time when space travel is as easy as air travel.

- Create a "Planet Trivia" game. Write facts about the planets on cards. Decorate a piece of cardboard to make a playing board and game pieces. Use the fact cards to review information about the planets and compete with other students. (Teacher: Revise the game for use with other book chapters.)

- Draw a picture (or make a model) of what you think a person from another planet would look like. Label the parts of the person's body that are different from ours and give a short explanation of what the part is and what it is used for (e.g., webbed feet: to assist in walking on the planet's sandy surface).

Chapter 3
The Moon

■ Teaching Resources

Books containing experiment(s) relating to the subject matter are marked with a plus sign (+) before and after the title.

P   *So That's How the Moon Changes Shape!*, by Allan Fowler (Children's Press, 1991)
A simple explanation of the moon and why it changes shape throughout the month.

P   *What the Moon Is Like*, by Franklyn M. Branley (Thomas Y. Crowell, 1986)
Imagines sights and experiences on a moon visit.

P   *When You Look up at the Moon,* by Alan Fowler (Children's Press, 1994)
A Rookie Read-About Science book that explains what you see when you look up into the night sky at the moon.

P/I *Where Does the Moon Go?*, by Sidney Rosen (Carolrhoda Books, 1992)
Follows the moon through its 28-day trip around the Earth and identifies its different phases.

I/U *+Science Project Ideas about the Moon,+* by Robert Gardner (Enslow, 1997)
Introduces the phases and other characteristics of the moon through a series of experiments.

■ Reading Selections

Books marked with an asterisk (*) before and after the title are related to activities in the activity sections of this chapter.

Buffalo Girls, by Bobette McCarthy (Pocket Books, 1995)
> An illustrated version of the traditional folk song, in which the Buffalo girls sing by starlight and dance by the light of the moon.

The Ghost-Eye Tree, by Bill Martin Jr. (Henry Holt, 1988)
> Walking down a dark, lonely road on an errand one night, a brother and sister argue over who is afraid of the dread Ghost-Eye tree.

Goodnight Moon, by Margaret Wise Brown (HarperCollins, 1991)
> A child wishes goodnight to each of the objects in the great green room: goodnight chairs, goodnight comb, and goodnight air.

The Goodnight Moon Room, by Margaret Wise Brown (Harper & Row, 1984)
> Before going to sleep, a little rabbit says goodnight to his bedroom. Features pop-up, movable, and lift-the-flap illustrations.

Grandfather Twilight, by Barbara Berger (Paper Star, 1996)
At day's end, Grandfather Twilight walks in the forest to perform his evening task, bringing the miracle of night to the world.

Happy Birthday, Moon!, by Frank Asch (Simon & Schuster, 2000)
When a bear discovers that the moon shares his birthday, he buys the moon a beautiful hat as a present.

Many Moons, by James Thurber (Harcourt Brace, 1998)
Although many try, only the court jester is able to fulfill Princess Lenore's wish for the moon.

Martha and the Nightbird, by Helena Clare Pittman (Hastings House, 1990)
A beautiful nightbird takes Martha on a magical ride through the night skies.

The Moon and I, by Betsy Byars (Beech Tree Books, 1996)
The author describes how she writes and recounts childhood anecdotes while describing humorous adventures with a blacksnake.

The Moon Jumpers, by Janice May Udry (HarperCollins, 1999)
A group of children enjoy playing in the moonlight.

The Moon Lake, by Ivan Gantschev (Neugebauer Press, 1996)
The moon lake helps a young boy keep the moon's bathing spot a secret from the greedy mayor and constables.

New Moon, by Pegi Deitz Shea (Boyds Mills Press, 1996)
A young girl looks for the moon on a dark winter night.

Owl Moon, by Jane Yolen (Philomel, 1988)
When the moon was full, a boy and his father stayed up late and went owling.

Papa, Please Get the Moon for Me, by Eric Carle (Little, Simon, 1999)
Monica's father fulfills her request for the moon by taking it down after it is small enough to carry, but it continues to change in size.

Regards to the Man in the Moon, by Ezra Jack Keats (Four Winds Press, 1981)
With the help of his imagination, his parents, and a few scraps of junk, Louie and his friends travel through space.

The Truth about the Moon, by Clayton Bess (Houghton Mifflin, 1992)
An African child is told several stories about the moon, but he still feels he has not learned the truth.

The Turtle and the Moon, by Charles Turner (Puffin Books, 1996)
A lonely turtle makes friends with the moon.

Under the Moon, by Dyan Sheldon (Dial Books for Young Readers, 1994)
After finding an arrowhead in her yard, a young girl has a dream about the Indians who once lived in the same area.

Wait till the Moon Is Full, by Margaret Wise Brown (Harper Trophy, 1989)
A little raccoon wants to see the night, but his mother makes him wait until the moon is full.

White Is the Moon, by Valerie Greeley (Macmillan, 1991)
Various colors are illustrated with poems for each color.

The following books are out of print, but may be available at the local library.

The Boy Who Ate the Moon, by Christopher King (Philomel Books, 1988)
> After eating the moon, a boy takes a strange journey.

Builder of the Moon, by Tim Wynne-Jones (McElderry Books, 1988)
> Brave block-builder David Finebloom receives a message from the moon that it is falling apart, so he rushes off to help.

Buried Moon, by Margaret Hodges (Little, Brown, 1990)
> Who will rescue the moon after she is buried in a deep pool by witches and goblins who have always resented her light?

The Buried Moon, by Amanda Walsh (Houghton Mifflin, 1991)
> The moon is held prisoner in the bog by the Hidden Folk, until the townspeople miss her light and go in search of her.

The Farmer and the Moon, by Anneliese Lussert (North-South Books, 1987)
> A poor farmer receives help from an unexpected source to teach a neighbor that greed has its price.

In Window Eight, the Moon is Late, by Diane Worfolk Allison (Little, Brown, 1988)
> At the end of a summer day, a little girl goes through the house saying good night to the various members of her family.

Little Daylight, by George MacDonald (North-South Books, 1987)
> At her christening, the princess, Little Daylight, receives a curse from a wicked fairy that she shall never see the sun and shall be affected by the changing moon until kissed by a prince.

Moonlight, by Jan Ormerod (Lothrop, Lee & Shepard, 1982)
> As her parents attempt to help a child fall asleep at bedtime, they themselves become more and more sleepy.

The Moon's Revenge, by Joan Aiken (Alfred A. Knopf, 1987)
> Seppy forces the moon to give him his wish, to be the maker of the enchanted fiddle music, but almost pays a horrible price for it. (Chapter Book)

Step Into the Night, by Joanne Ryder (Four Winds Press, 1988)
> A child stands outside her moonlit home and imagines the lives of many night creatures as they move silently in the unseen world of darkness.

Under the Moon, by Joanne Ryder (Random House, 1989)
> Mama mouse teaches her little mouse how to tell where home is by reminding her of its special smells, sounds, and textures.

What Rhymes with Moon?, by Jane Yolen (Philomel Books, 1993)
> Contains nineteen poems that relate to the moon.

■ Science Activities

Sequencing

Read *Many Moons* by Thurber to the class. Write the different events that happened in the story on separate index cards. Mix up the cards and have the student(s) put the cards in order.

Ratios/Percentages

Tell the students that the moon's gravity is about 17 percent of the Earth's. Ask them to figure out what the following objects would weigh on the moon:

5-pound bag of sugar (0.85 lb.)

175-pound person (29.75 lbs.)

25-pound dog (4.25 lbs.)

40-pound chair (6.8 lbs.)

1,800-pound car (306 lbs.)

Phases of the Moon

Have the students draw a picture showing how the moon looks in the night sky one night. Repeat this exercise every night for the following 14 to 21 days. Ask the students to describe how the moon is changing, and why. Have the students make flipbooks by stapling together 28 small sheets of paper. Each day, they should draw the moon as it appears that evening. Students should make the moon the same size and in approximately the same spot on the page each day. When the books are completed, they can flip the pages and watch the moon change.

Time Capsule

Ask students to imagine that they are traveling on the space shuttle to the moon. They and the crew are to leave a "time capsule" on the moon that represents the Earth, the United States, and them, personally. What items would they put in the time capsule? Why did they choose these items?

NASA

Have students research the United States (NASA's) manned space flights to the moon, looking for answers to the following questions: What kind of scientific research were the astronauts to carry out? Was their mission a success? Why was space exploration to the moon discontinued?

Moon Map

Have students use one of the books from the "Teaching Resources" section (or an encyclopedia) to draw a map of the moon's surface. They should label the moon's craters and other areas that have been given names. Students could make this map out of dough and use markers to label it.

■ Creative Writing Activities

Following are instructions to give the students for various writing activities.

- Would you like to live on the moon someday? Write about how your life would be different there than on Earth. (More advanced students could compose a letter to their representative or senator in Congress requesting to be part of the first settlement on the moon. Have them state reasons why they would be a good choice.)

- Read *Builder of the Moon* by Wynne-Jones. What if David had not been able to help the moon? Write a different ending for the story.

- Imagine you are looking through a telescope placed on the moon, observing the Earth below. Write and illustrate what you see.

- Read *In Window Eight, the Moon Is Late* by Allison. Write a similar book describing what you see out of different windows of your house.

- Write a description of the moon that you could use to help someone who is blind "see" it for the first time. Be sure to include a description of the different phases of the moon.

- Read *Moonlight* by Ormerod. Choose one page of the book and write a story to go along with the pictures.

- Write a story about the "Man in the Moon." How did he get there, and why does his face look like it does?

- Imagine what it would have been like to be the first person on the moon. What would you like to bring back to Earth with you? Would you leave anything on the moon for future explorers to find? Imagine that a baby animal from the moon stows away on your return flight to Earth. What is this animal like? What does it eat? Can it adapt to life on Earth? Write a story about either of these ideas or write a story that encompasses both ideas.

■ Art Activities

Following are instructions to give the students for various art activities.

- If you were to give the moon a hat for a birthday present, what would it look like? Design your own hat. (Draw it or use construction paper, markers, glitter, etc., to "make" a hat.) (*Happy Birthday, Moon!* by Asch)

- Sing the song, "Buffalo Girls Won't You Come Out Tonight." Create your own "dance by the light of the moon." (*Buffalo Girls* by McCarthy).

- Go rock collecting. When you get home with your "collection," wash the rocks and decorate them (with paint, markers, glitter, etc.) to make your own "moon rocks."

- Create a rocket ship from a large cardboard box. Glue on spools, jar lids, bottle caps or mirrors for the instrument panel. Cut out a window. Make a helmet from a bowl or a pot. Sit down and buckle up! Have a nice trip to the moon! (*Regards to the Man in the Moon* by Keats)

- Give the "Man in the Moon" a new face (or create many different faces to fit different moods). How does he look tonight? Is he happy, sad, or angry?

- Draw a picture of your room. What objects would you say goodnight to at the end of the day? (*Goodnight Moon* by Brown)

- Write and illustrate your own book of colors, starting with the pages: "White is the moon"; "Yellow is the sun"; "Blue is the . . . " (*White Is the Moon* by Greeley)

- Create a dance and demonstrate it as if you are dancing on the moon. Remember that there is less gravity on the moon.

- Draw a picture illustrating the phrase "Moonlight Madness." Use any image that comes to your mind (a person turning into a werewolf or a vampire, unusual woodland activities during a full moon, crazed shoppers stampeding a store, etc.).

Chapter 4
Space Exploration

■ Teaching Resources

Books containing experiment(s) relating to the subject matter are marked with a plus sign (+) before and after the title.

P   *A Day in Space,* by Suzanne Lord and Jolie Epstein (Scholastic, 1986)
Describes what it would be like to go up in the space shuttle.

P/I   *Spacecraft,* by Ian Graham (Steck-Vaughn, 1995)
A history of space vehicles.

I   *Moonwalk: The First Trip to the Moon,* by Judy Donnelly (Random House, 1989)
Narrates the preparations and activities that resulted in the first landing of humans on the moon in July 1969.

I   *Space Sailing,* by D. M. Souza (Lerner, 1994)
Discusses how sunlight can be used to propel spacecraft equipped with sails to reach destinations beyond the reach of conventional crafts.

I   *To Space and Back,* by Sally Ride with Susan Okie (Lothrop, Lee & Shepard, 1989)
Describes in text and photographs what it is like to be an astronaut on the space shuttle.

I/U *The Mission to Mars and Beyond,* by Vincent V. DeSomma (Chelsea House, 1991)
Discusses the proposed manned space flight to Mars and what might be found there.

U   *Mars Landing and the Viking,* by Gregory Vogt (Millbrook Press, 1991)
The story of the Viking mission, the events that led up to it, and what we found out about Mars.

U   *Millions of Miles to Mars,* by Joseph W. Kelch (Silver Burdett, 1995)
Describes the recent journey to the red planet by the Viking spacecraft.

■ Reading Selections

Books marked with an asterisk (*) before and after the title are related to activities in the activity sections of this chapter.

Aliens for Breakfast, by Jonathan Etra and Stephanie Spinner (Random House, 1988)
Finding an intergalactic special agent in his cereal box, Richard joins in a fight to save Earth from the Dranes, one of whom is masquerading as a student in Richard's school. (Also available are *Aliens for Dinner,* 1994; *Aliens for Lunch,* 1991.) (Chapter Book)

The Berenstain Bears on the Moon, by Stan Berenstain (Random House, 1985)
Two Berenstain Bears and their pup take a rocket ship to the moon.

Destination Moon, by Herge (Little, Brown, 1988)
Tintin, Snowy, and Captain Haddock join Professor Calculus's moon expedition.

Explorers on the Moon, by Herge (Little, Brown, 1988)
Tintin and his friends are involved in the first manned flight to the moon that proves perilous.

The Forgotten Door, by Alexander Key (Scholastic, 1989)
Jon falls through the forgotten door to the strange planet Earth. He makes friends with a local family, but must find the secret passage quickly to return home. (Chapter Book)

Gorky Rises, by William Steig (Sunburst, 1986)
While basking in the sun, Gorky falls asleep and wakes to find himself floating in the immense sky. Orbiting the globe can have its ups and downs, and Gorky wonders if he'll ever get back to Earth.

Harold's Trip to the Sky, by Crockett Johnson (HarperCollins Juvenile Books, 1981)
Harold travels to the sky with the help of his purple crayon.

Mooncake, by Frank Asch (Aladdin, 1988)
Bear builds a rocket to take him to the moon so he can taste it.

Professor Noah's Spaceship, by Brian Wildsmith (Oxford University Press, 1985)
As the forest begins to change, the animals and birds, no longer happy there, fly away in Professor Noah's amazing spaceship.

Strange Orbit, by Margaret Simpson (State University of New York Press, 1995)
Fourteen-year-old Jessica is chosen to go to the moon, but the spaceship goes off course and sends the crew on a mysterious voyage through space. (Chapter Book)

When the Tripods Came, by John Christopher (Aladdin, 1990)
Fourteen-year-old Laurie and his family attempt to flee England when the Tripods descend from outer space and begin brainwashing everyone. (Chapter Book)

The following books are out of print, but may be available at the local library.

*Alistair in Outer Space,** by Marilyn Sadler (Prentice-Hall, 1984)
When Alistair is kidnapped by a spaceship full of Goots from Gootula, his main concern is for his overdue library books.

Black Suits from Outer Space, by Gene De Weese (G. P. Putnam's Sons, 1985)
Two young people meet a visitor from outer space who badly needs their help. (Chapter Book)

Cosmic Chickens, by Ned Delaney (Harper & Row, 1988)
Three chickens from outer space help Hank save his farm from the greedy Mr. Sneezle.

I Spent My Summer Vacation Kidnapped into Space, by Martyn N. Godfrey (Scholastic, 1990)
Reeann and her friend, Jared, are kidnapped by Torkan aliens and taken to the planet, Freetal, to provide entertainment for the aliens. (Chapter Book)

It Came from Outer Space, by Tony Bradman (Dial Books, 1992)
A visitor from outer space visits an elementary school class and brings an important message about physical beauty.

The Package in Hyperspace, by Janet Asimov (Walker, 1988)
> Twelve-year-old Ginnela and her younger brother, Pete, find themselves trapped on a disabled spaceship and must figure out how to survive. (Chapter Book)

The Planetoid of Amazement, by Mel Gilden (HarperCollins, 1991)
> Following strange instructions that come in the mail, Rodney meets two aliens who are collecting artifacts for an intergalactic museum, the House of Amazements on Hutzenklutz Stations. (Chapter Book)

UFO Diary, by Satoshi Kitamura (Farrar, Straus & Giroux, 1989)
> A UFO lost in space spots a strange, blue planet and its inhabitants find a new friend there.

Wanted: UFO, by Beatrice Gormley (Dutton Children's Books, 1990)
> Fifth-grader, Elise, is thrilled when a UFO appears in her friend's backyard, but shocked when she discovers why its occupants have come to Earth. (Chapter Book)

■ Science Activities

Planet Travel

Tell students that the class is going on a trip to Mars (or to one of the other planets). Have them research the planet to determine how long it will take you to get there; what supplies you will need to take with you, and what you will do when you get there.

Astronomers/Astronauts

- Have students choose a specific astronomer or astronaut and research his or her life.
- Depending on the age of your students, have them write a summary of the astronomer's life and discoveries; draw a picture of the astronomer and the planet, constellation, or other bodies he or she discovered; or put together a play about the highlights of the astronomer's life.
- Depending on the age of your students, have them write a summary of the astronaut's life and space journeys; draw a picture of the astronaut on a space mission; or put together a play or book depicting the astronaut, the training he or she went through, and the resulting space travel.

Earth Speedometer

- Have students make an Earth speedometer to clock the Earth's speed as it spins. They will each need the following supplies: a magnifying glass, masking tape, a chair, a piece of white paper, and a watch/clock with a second hand.
- Have the students tape the handle of the magnifying glass to the seat of the chair so that the lens extends horizontally over the edge of the seat, then place the chair in the sun. They should put the paper on the floor under the magnifying glass where the light shines after passing through the lens and adjust the chair and/or paper until the sunlight causes a sharp circle of light on the paper.
- Tell students to draw a circle around the spot of light, then use the watch or clock to time how long it takes for the sunlight to completely leave the circle.
- Explain that the spot of light is a little picture of the sun. When the light has moved completely out of the circles they drew, the Earth has traveled half of 1 degree of the 360 degrees that it rotates in a "day's" time. Have the students multiply the time it took for the light to move out of their circle by 720 and convert the answer into hours (divide by 60). They will figure out approximately how long a "day" really is.

Satellites

Tell students that there are many objects in orbit around the Earth right now. Have them research satellites in general (how they get into space, why they were put into space, how they function, how long they last in space). You may want to have a more advanced student pick a particular satellite to research and report on.

Planetarium

Take a field trip to the local planetarium. (Call beforehand to see what the topic of the current exhibit is and to schedule your class.) Many planetariums have educational programs that can fit into your curriculum.

Make a Rocket

Bring in the following to make a rocket, as a class:

One 2-liter soda bottle

A rectangular piece of cardboard

A bicycle air pump

A cork to fit snuggly into the neck of the soda bottle

A needle used to pump up a basketball

A nail

Water

Some masking tape or duct tape

- Wash out the soda bottle and then fill it one-fourth of the way with water.
- Cut the cardboard into four rectangles (3 inches wide by 7 inches long). Then cut the lower left-hand corner of each rectangle to conform to the shape of the soda bottle (at the neck end of the bottle). Tape these "fins" to the bottle, an equal distance apart, to make the fins that your rocket will rest on before launching.
- Take the nail and make a hole down through the middle of the cork just big enough so that the needle will fit in it snuggly. Put the needle in the cork, then push the cork snuggly into the neck of the soda bottle.
- Connect the bicycle air pump to the needle and stand your rocket upside-down, on its fins. Begin pumping air into the bottle through the needle. When the air pressure inside the bottle gets strong enough, it will force the cork out of the neck and your rocket will soar into space.
- *Warning:* Be sure that you launch your rocket outside because the water inside the bottle will spray out when the cork ejects. Also, be sure everyone is standing a safe distance from the bottle so that it does not strike anyone when it launches.

■ Creative Writing Activities

Following are instructions to give the students for various writing activities.

- Write a letter to an astronaut. What questions would you ask? You will need to do some research on the astronaut you choose before beginning your letter.
- Imagine that you are an astronaut. How does it feel living in a space capsule for such a long period of time? What do you miss most about the Earth? What do you miss the least? Write down your feelings in journal form as a record of your journey.

- You have been accepted as a passenger on the next space shuttle flight! However, as the time for departure draws near, you change your mind and don't want to take the trip. Write a letter to the head of NASA explaining why you no longer want to take the flight.

- You have traveled to a distant planet and are now experiencing weightlessness. How are things different? Write a description of someone trying to perform a task, such as cooking dinner, in a weightless environment.

- You have traveled to a new planet that is inhabited. What are these inhabitants like? How do they entertain you during your visit? Write a thank-you letter to your new friends for the wonderful visit you had.

- A satellite has fallen from its orbit and landed in your backyard. Write a story about what it looks like and how you find out where it came from. Why was it in space? What made it fall?

- You have been asked to head an expedition that will establish the first colony on the moon. You need to outfit the entire expedition. What type of people would you ask to go with you? What knowledge and skills should they have? What supplies would you take with you? What type of housing would you need to use? Start a journal documenting the decision-making process you use to outfit your expedition. Write a letter to a friend telling of your groups' experiences during your first three months on the moon.

■ Art Activities

Following are instructions to give the students for various art activities.

- You get to choose the song that will wake up the astronauts on their first day in space. What will it be? Why? Write your own song (to a familiar melody) that would be good to wake up the astronauts.

- Make up an advertising poster to recruit people interested in becoming astronauts for NASA.

- Build a model rocket ship using assorted sizes of tin cans or plastic containers. Paint your rocket ship and design an emblem for your space organization.

- Draw a picture of a space traveler from another planet. What would he or she look like? What type of spacesuit and equipment would the traveler have? What would the spaceship be like? You can also use household items to make the spacecraft.

- Pretend that you are the inhabitant of another planet in outer space. Write the words for your national anthem. If you model it after a song you know, you can actually sing your song for your family.

- Make up your own planet. Draw what the terrain would look like (the color of the sky, ground, etc.). Include the planet's plant life, animals, and people in your picture. Draw a city on your planet. Draw the vehicles commonly used on your planet.

- Send a satellite into space that will deliver a message to the universe. What will your message be? Draw a picture of your creation and write a story about why you felt this message was necessary. How did everyone react to your satellite?

- You are one of the first people to live on the moon. How will you decorate your bedroom? Will your room look like a traditional bedroom on Earth or be very different? Which of your possessions will you bring from Earth? Draw a picture of your new room.

■ Experiment Books

Aviation and Space Science Projects, by Dr. Ben Millspaugh (TAB Books, 1992)
> Includes projects on aviation and space-related subjects such as air density, wind, balloons, gliders, and spacecraft.

More Mudpies to Magnets, by Elizabeth A. Sherwood, Robert A. Williams, and Robert E. Rockwell (Gryphon House, 1991)
> A collection of experiments for young children on the subjects of space, plants, and animals.

Science for Kids: 39 Easy Astronomy Experiments, by Robert W. Wood (TAB Books, 1991)
> Contains 39 experiments dealing with such things as measuring celestial bodies, making a spectroscope and telescope, photographing star tracks, gravity, and growing plants in space.

Talking to Fireflies, Shrinking the Moon, by Edward Duensing (Fulcrum, 1997)
> Describes many different things you can do with your children to heighten their interest in nature and creation (and yours, too!).

■ Organizations

Astronomy

Local Societies

American Association of Variable
Star Astronomers
187 Concord Ave.
Tucson, AZ 85732

Astronomical League
c/o Carole J. Beaman, Editor
The Reflector
6804 Alvina Road
Rockford, IL 61103

Astronomical League
Donald Archer, Exec. Sec.
P.O. Box 12821
Cambridge, MA 02138

Teaching Resources

MMI Space Science Corp.
Dept. ST-85
2950 Wymann Pkwy.
P.O. Box 19907
Baltimore, MD 21211

1985 Astronomy Resource Guide
West Virginia University Bookstore
College Ave.
Morgantown, WV 26506

The Night Sky Company
1334 Brommer St.
Santa Cruz, CA 95062

General Information

Astro Cards (observation aids)
P.O. Box 35
Natrona Heights, PA 15065

Astro Tech
101 W. Main
P.O. Box 2001
Ardmore, OK 73402
observation aids

Astronomical Society of the Pacific
Tapes Department
1290 24th Ave.
San Francisco, CA 94122
cassettes and maps for star gazing

The Department of Physics
Furman University
Greenville, SC 29613

Edmund Mag 5 Star Atlas
Edmund Scientific
101 E. Gloucester Pike
Barrington, NJ 08007
star charts

Everything in the Universe
5248 Lawton Ave.
Oakland, CA 94618
observation aids

National Space Society
600 Maryland Ave. S.W.
Washington, D.C. 20024

Peninsula Scientific
2185 Park Blvd.
Palo Alto, CA 94306
observation aids

The Planetary Society
65 North Catalina
Pasadena, CA 91106

Sky Atlas 2000.0
Sky Publishing Corporation
49 Bay State Rd.
Cambridge, MA 02238
star charts

National Aeronautics and Space Administration (NASA) Teacher Resource Centers

Ames Research Center
Teacher Resource Center
Mail Stop 204-7
Greenbelt, MD 20771
415-694-6077

Goddard Space Flight Center
Teacher Resource Center
Mail Code 130.3
Moffet Field, CA 94035
301-344-8981

Jet Propulsion Laboratory
Science & Math Teaching Resource
Center
c/o Education Outreach-MSTRC
Mail Stop 520
Pasadena, CA 91109
818-354-4321

Johnson Space Center
Teacher Resource Center AP4
Houston, TX 77058
713-783-3455

Kennedy Space Center
Educator Resource Library
Mail Code ERL
Kennedy Space Center, FL 32899
305-867-4090

Langley Research Center
Teacher Resource Center
Mail Stop 146
Hampton, VA 23665
804-865-4468

Lewis Research Center
Teacher Resource Center
Mail Stop 8-1
Cleveland, OH 44135
216-267-1187

Marshall Space Flight Center
Teacher Resource Center
Space and Rocket Center
Tranquility Base
Huntsville, AL 35812
205-837-3400, ext. 36

National Space Technology Lab
Teacher Resource Center
Building 1200
NSTL Station, MS 39529
601-688-3338

The Moon

NASA Kennedy Space Center
Educational Services Office
Kennedy Space Center, FL 32899
information on missions to the moon;
catalogs of posters, slides, and astronomical materials

Selectory Sales
Astronomical Society of the Pacific
1290 24th Ave.
San Francisco, CA 94122

Space Communications Branch
Ministry of State for Science and Technology
240 Sparks St.
C.D. Howe Building
Ottawa, Ontario K1A 1A1
Canada

STARDATE
MacDonald Observatory
Austin, TX 78712

The Milky Way and Other Galaxies

AstroMedia Order Department
1027 N. 7th St.
Milwaukee, WI 53233
catalogs of slides, posters, and
astronomy materials

Caltech Bookstore
California Institute of Technology
Mail Code 1-51
Pasadena, CA 91125
photography of galaxies

Sky Publishing Corporation
49 Bay State Rd.
Cambridge, MT 02238-1290
catalogs of slides, posters, and astronomy
materials

The Planets

Scientific & Technical Information
Office
Jet Propulsion Laboratory
California Institute of Technology
Pasadena, CA 91109
The Voyage of Mariner 10

Scientific & Technical Information Office
National Aeronautics & Space Administration
Washington, D.C. 20546
Atlas of Mercury, The Martian Landscape,
Viking Orbiter Views of Mars

Special Sources of Books and Equipment

American Science Center
5700 Northwest Highway
Chicago, IL 60646

AstroMedia
P.O. Box 92788
Milwaukee, WI 53202

Book Faire
Sky Publications Corp.
49-62 Bay State Rd.
Cambridge, MA 02238-1290

Earth Science Materials
P.O. Box 69
Florence, CO 81226

Fisher Scientific Company
Educational Division
4901 W. LeMoyne St.
Chicago, IL 60651

Frey Scientific Company
905 Hickory Lane
Mansfield, OH 44905

Macmillan Scientific Company
8200 S. Hoyne Ave.
Chicago, IL 60620

Orion Telescope Center
P.O. Box 158
Santa Cruz, CA 95061

Ward's Natural Science Establishment
P.O. Box 1712
Rochester, NY 14603

Miscellaneous

International Scientific and Engineering
Fair
Science Service
1719 N. St., N.W.
Washington, D.C. 20036

Space Shuttle Student Involvement Project
National Science Teachers Association
1742 Connecticut Ave., N.W.
Washington, D.C. 20009

Westinghouse Science Talent Search
Science Service
1719 N. St., N.W.
Washington, D.C. 20036

■ Magazines/Periodicals

The Astrograph
P.O. Box 2283
Arlington, VA 22202

Astronomy
Astromedia Corporation
1027 N. 7th St.
Milwaukee, WI 53233

Comet News Service
P.O. Box TDR, No. 92
Truckee, CA 95734

Journal of the ALPO
Association of Lunar & Planetary Observers
P.O. Box 16131
San Francisco, CA 94116

McDonald Observatory News
The University of Texas
McDonald Observatory
Room RLM 15.308
Austin, TX 78712
monthly newsletter with current
sky charts

Odyssey
Astromedia Corporation
1027 N. 7th St.
Milwaukee, WI 53233

Mercury
Astronomical Society of the Pacific
1290 24th Ave.
San Francisco, CA 94122

Sky and Telescope
Sky Publishing Corporation
49 Bay State Rd.
Cambridge, MA 02238

Meteor News
c/o Wanda Simmons
Rt. 3, Box 424-99
Calahan, FL 32011

Sky Calendar
Abrams Planetarium
Michigan State University
East Lansing, MI 48824
monthly sky calendar and evening skies

The Observer's Handbook: Yearly Periodical
The Royal Astronomical Society of Canada
124 Merton St.
Toronto M4S 2Z2, Canada

■ Additional Reading

The Genesis Flood, by John C. Whitcomb and Henry M. Morris (Grand Rapids, MI: Baker Book House, 1989).

The Genesis Record, by Henry M. Morris (Grand Rapids, MI: Baker Book House, 1981).

Great Lives: Sally Ride Shooting for the Stars, by Jane Hurwitz and Sue Hurwitz (New York: Fawcett Columbine, 1989).

The New Patterns in the Sky: Myths and Legends of the Stars, by Julius D. W. Staal (Blacksburg, VA: McDonald & Woodward, 1996).

Ronald McNair: Astronaut, by Corinne Naden (New York: Chelsea House, 1991).

What Is Creation Science?, by Henry M. Morris and Gary E. Parker (El Cajon, CA: Master Books, 1987).

■ Web Sites

The following Web sites reference additional Web sites relating to the solar system and space. These Web sites were created especially for children. All sites were accessed in March 2001 and were active at that time.

Astronauts: http://www.yahooligans.com/science_and_oddities/the_Earth/Space/astronauts

Constellations and stars: http://www.yahooligans.com/science_and_oddities/the_Earth/Space/Astronomy/

NASA: http://www.yahooligans.com/science_and_oddities/the_Earth/Space/NASA

Northern Lights: http://www.yahooligans.com/science_and_oddities/the_Earth/Space/Astronomy/Northern_lights

Planets of the Solar System: http://www.yahooligans.com/science_and_oddities/the_Earth/Space/Astronomy/Solar_system

Satellites: http://www.yahooligans.com/science_and_oddities/the_Earth/Space/Satellites

Space stations: http://www.yahooligans.com/science_and_oddities/the_Earth/Space/Space_Stations

UFOs: http://www.yahooligans.com/science_and_oddities/the_Earth/Space/UFOs

The following web sites discuss a specific topic about the solar system:

Adler Planetarium: http://astro.uchicago.edu/adler/

Astronomical Society of the Pacific: http://www.aspsky.org/

Astronomy for Small Children: http://starchild.gsfc.nasa.gov/

Aurora Borealis: http://www.geo.mtu.edu/weather/aurora/

Charles Messier's Database: http://seds.lpl.arizona.edu/messier/Messier.html

Comet and meteor information: http://spacelink.msfc.nasa.gov/Instructional.Materials/

Comets and meteors: http://www.noao.edu/education/igcomet/igcomet.html

Hubble Space Telescope photos: http://antwrp.gsfc.nasa.gov/apod/astropix.html

Johnson Space Center's photos: http://images.jsc.nasa.gov

NASA photographs: http:///pds.jpl.nasa.gov/planets/

Planet pictures: http://seds.lpl.arizona.edu.nineplanets/nineplanets/nineplanets.html

Sky and Telescope magazine: http://www.skypub.com

Space shuttle launches: http://www.ksc.nasa.gov/shuttle/missions/missions.html

Sun facts: http://seds.lpl.arizona.edu/nineplanets/nineplanets/sol.html

Index

About the Authors

Amy J. Bain is a teacher in the Miami Elementary School system, Milford, Ohio, and is president of Solomon Publishing. **Janet Richer** has worked extensively writing and presenting training workshops and videos for homeschooling families throughout the Midwest. **Janet Weckman** is a teacher at Blanche Moore Elementary School, Corpus Christi, Texas, with more than 20 years of teaching experience, including working with hearing-impaired students.

from *Teacher Ideas Press*

CELEBRATING THE EARTH: Stories, Experiences, Activities
Norma J. Livo

Invite young readers to observe, explore, and appreciate the natural world through engaging activities. Livo shows you how to use folk stories, personal narrative, and a variety of learning projects to teach students about amphibians, reptiles, mammals, constellations, plants, and other natural phenomena. Designed to build a Naturalist Intelligence in young learners, these stories and activities are packed with scientific information. **All Levels.**
xvii, 174p. 8½x11 paper ISBN 1-56308-776-6

FAMOUS PROBLEMS AND THEIR MATHEMATICIANS
Art Johnson

Why did ordering an omelet cost one mathematician his life? The answer to this and other questions are found in this exciting new resource that shows your students how 60 mathematicians discovered mathematical solutions through everyday situations. These lessons are easily incorporated into the curriculum as an introduction to a math concept, a homework piece, or an extra challenge. Teacher notes and suggestions for the classroom are followed by extension problems and additional background material. **Grades 5–12.**
xvi, 179p. 8½x11 paper ISBN 1-56308-446-5

SCIENCE AND MATH BOOKMARK BOOK: 300 Fascinating, Fact-Filled Bookmarks
Kendall Haven and Roni Berg

Use these 300 reproducible bookmarks of fascinating facts, concepts, trivia, inventions, and discoveries to spark student learning. They cover all major disciplines of math and physical, earth, and life sciences—ready to copy, cut out, and give to your students. **Grades 4 and up.**
xii, 115p. 8½x11 paper ISBN 1-56308-675-1

WRITE RIGHT! Creative Writing Using Storytelling Techniques
Kendall Haven

Haven's breakthrough approach to creative writing uses storytelling techniques to enhance the creative writing process. This practical guide offers you directions for 38 writing exercises that will show students how to create powerful and dynamic fiction. All the steps are included, from finding inspiration and creating believable characters to the final edit. Activities are coded by levels, but most can be adapted to various grades. **All Levels.**
240p. 8½x11 paper ISBN 1-56308-677-8

VISUAL MESSAGES: Integrating Imagery into Instruction
2d Edition
David M. Considine and Gail E. Haley

The authors provide effective media literacy strategies, activities, and resources that help students learn the critical-viewing skills necessary in our media-dominated world. Various media and types of programs are addressed, including motion pictures, television news, and advertising. Activities are coded by grade level and curriculum area. **Grades K–12.**
xxiii,371p. 8½x11 paper ISBN 1-56308-575-5

For a free catalog or to place an order, please contact:
Teacher Ideas Press
Dept. B051 • P.O. Box 6633 • Englewood, CO • 80155-6633
800-237-6124 • www.lu.com/tip • Fax: 303-220-8843